THE DECLINING
SIGNIFICANCE
OF RACE

THE DECLINING SIGNIFICANCE OF RACE

Blacks and Changing American Institutions

WILLIAM JULIUS WILSON

THE UNIVERSITY OF CHICAGO PRESS
Chicago and London

WILLIAM JULIUS WILSON is professor and chairman of the Department of Sociology at the University of Chicago. He is the author of *Power, Racism, and Privilege: Race Relations in Theoretical and Sociohistorical Perspectives* and the coeditor of *Through Different Eyes: Black and White Perspectives on American Race Relations.* He was named a 1977 Sidney Spivak Fellow of Inter-group Relations by the American Sociological Association.

The University of Chicago Press, Chicago 60637
The University of Chicago Press, Ltd., London

Portions of chapters 1 and 3 in this book appeared in slightly different form in William J. Wilson, "Class Conflict and Jim Crow Segregation in the Postbellum South," *Pacific Sociological Review* 19, no. 4 (October 1976), pp. 431–46) and are used by permission of the publisher, Sage Publications, Inc.; portions of chapter 5 appeared in William J. Wilson, "The Changing Context of American Race Relations," in *Case Studies on Human Rights and Fundamental Freedoms: A World Survey,* vol. 5, pp. 175–96, © copyright 1976 by Martinus Nijhoff; one section of chapter 5 draws on William J. Wilson, "The Significance of Social and Racial Prisms," in *Through Different Eyes,* ed. Peter I. Rose, Stanley Rothman, and William J. Wilson, © copyright 1973 by Oxford University Press.

Library of Congress Cataloging in Publication Data

Wilson, William J   1935–
   The declining significance of race.

   Bibliography: p.
   Includes index.
   1. United States—Race relations. 2. Afro-Americans—Economic conditions. 3. Afro-Americans—Social conditions. I. Title.
E185.W73   301.45′1′0973   77–10551
ISBN 0–226–90128–9

To Carter, Colleen, Lisa, and Paula

CONTENTS

This book is a study of race and class in the American experience. Its focus is a rather significant departure from that of my previous book, *Power, Racism, and Privilege*, in which I paid little attention to the role of class in understanding issues of race. I now feel that many important features of black and white relations in America are not captured when the issue is defined as majority versus minority and that a preoccupation with race and racial conflict obscures fundamental problems that derive from the intersection of class with race. I should hasten to point out, however, that I do not subscribe to the view that racial problems are necessarily derived from the more fundamental economic class problems. The issues are far more complex than such an analysis would suggest. When black and white relations are viewed from a broad historical perspective, a uniform reliance on class to explain all forms and degrees of racial conflict can be as misleading as a uniform reliance on race.

Since "class" is a slippery concept that has been defined in a variety of ways in the social science literature, I should like to indicate that in this study the concept means any group of people who have more or less similar goods, services, or skills to offer for income in a given economic order and who therefore receive similar financial remuneration in the marketplace. One's economic class position determines in major measure one's life chances, including the chances for external living conditions and personal life experiences.*

It is appropriate to point out in this connection that in a racist society—that is, a society in which the major institutions are regulated by racist ideology—the economic class position of individual minorities is heavily determined by race. In such a society the life chances of the members of individual minorities are essentially more a function of race than of class. However, as the influence of race on minority class-stratification decreases, then, of course, class takes on greater importance in determining the life chances of minority individuals. The clear and growing class divisions among blacks today constitute a case in point. It is difficult to speak of a uniform black experience when the black population can be meaningfully stratified into groups whose members range from those who are affluent to those who are impoverished. This of course has not always been the case, because the crystallization of a black class structure is fairly recent.

In this study I have traced the development of a black class structure and have related it to what I perceive to be the declining influence of race in the economic sector. In chapter 6, following E. Franklin Frazier's lead, I have associated the black middle class with those who are employed in white-collar jobs and in craftsmen and foremen positions. The problem with this broad classification, insofar as it relates to my definition of economic class, is that although the positions of professional and technical workers, proprietors, managers and officials, and clerical workers all show yearly median incomes that exceed those of semiskilled operatives, service workers, unskilled laborers, and farm workers, this is not true of the white-collar position of sales workers. The median income of black sales workers in 1973 was below that of semiskilled operatives and roughly equivalent to that of unskilled laborers and service workers. However, even as late as 1973, only 2 percent of all black workers were classified as sales workers and therefore their inclusion in the broad white-collar category does not seriously distort either my definition of the black middle class or my description and analysis of the changing black class structure.

It could be suggested that the black class structure is only a truncated version of the white class structure because the average

*This conception of "class" is a modified version of Max Weber's explication of the concept. See *From Max Weber: Essays in Sociology,* edited, with an introduction, by Hans Gerth and C. Wright Mills (New York: Oxford University Press, 1946), pp. 181–82.

income of black middle-class workers is uniformly lower than the average income of the white middle classes. However, this is a consequence of the historic effects of racial discrimination by which older black workers were denied entry into higher-paying white- and blue-collar positions. Since the progressive movement of the more educated blacks into the higher-paying middle-class jobs is being experienced primarily by the younger segments of the population, the income discrepancies between black and white workers is basically a reflection of differences in seniority. Despite the average income differences between black and white workers, it is clear that economic divisions now exist among blacks, divisions which show every sign of deepening and which have profound implications for the significance of race in the American experience.

The elaboration of a black class structure and a consideration of its social and racial implications are related to more general issues involving the relationships between race and class on the one hand, and basic institutions of American society on the other. The first chapter of this book outlines this relationship in terms of a broad theoretical framework that examines racial change from a macrosociological perspective. Chapter 2 analyzes the effect of a preindustrial system of production on the pattern of race relations in the antebellum South and details the changing relations between slaves and slaveholders. Chapter 3 focuses on different forms of racial antagonisms in the preindustrial and early industrial periods in relation to issues of class and class conflict. Chapter 4 considers the impact of industrialization on the changing patterns of race and class relations in the North from the turn of the century to World War II. Chapter 5 analyzes the modern industrial period of race relations, giving particular attention to the role of structural changes in the economy and the political changes of the state in displacing racial antagonisms from the economic sector to social, political, and community concerns and in creating vastly different mobility opportunities for different segments of the black population. Chapter 6 relates the development of a black class structure in the industrial and the modern industrial period to basic economic and political changes, shows the connection between social class and different types of black protest movements, and examines the relevance of increasing black urban political power in declining central cities. Finally, chapter 7 discusses the declining significance of race vis-à-vis basic theoretical and substantive arguments advanced in the previous chapters and attempts to redefine some of the problems that are generally perceived as racial in nature.

In the preparation of this book, I am deeply indebted to the University of Chicago for granting me a leave of absence during the 1975 academic year. A good portion of the manuscript was written during that period. I would like to give my special thanks to my former research assistant, Katherine O'Sullivan See, now an assistant professor of sociology at James Madison College of Michigan State University. She not only labored long hours in the University of Chicago library searching out obscure documents, but she was also a useful critic of and sounding board for my ideas. I would also like to thank Earline Franklin for her masterful job of typing the manuscript and suggesting appropriate editorial corrections.

I owe a very special debt to a number of people who read various versions of the manuscript. I am particularly grateful to Peter I. Rose, whose comments in 1975 on an early draft of the manuscript convinced me that my thinking on the subject had not sufficiently crystallized. I returned to the drawing board and produced the present version, which he read in its entirety and for which he provided useful comments and criticisms. Margaret Andersen, Edna Bonacich, Michael Burawoy, Jan Dizard, Nathan Glazer, Morris Janowitz, Ira Katznelson, Lewis Killian, Pierre van den Berghe, and Doris Wilkinson also read the entire manuscript and presented detailed written suggestions and criticisms that were extremely helpful in my final revisions. Parts of individual chapters were read by Richard Ogles and Loretta Williams, and they too provided helpful comments.

Finally, I would like to express my deepest appreciation to my wife, Beverly, who despite the omnipresence of both an energetic toddler and an inquisitive preschooler, carefully edited the entire manuscript and monitored the logical flow of my arguments. Moreover, she shielded me as best she could from outside pressures during my writing periods and provided emotional support with her unwavering enthusiasm for my arguments, even those that were only in their vaguest formulation.

1 FROM RACIAL OPPRESSION TO ECONOMIC CLASS SUBORDINATION

Race relations in America have undergone fundamental changes in recent years, so much so that now the life chances of individual blacks have more to do with their economic class position than with their day-to-day encounters with whites. In earlier years the systematic efforts of whites to suppress blacks were obvious to even the most insensitive observer. Blacks were denied access to valued and scarce resources through various ingenious schemes of racial exploitation, discrimination, and segregation, schemes that were reinforced by elaborate ideologies of racism. But the situation has changed. However determinative such practices were for the previous efforts of the black population to achieve racial equality, and however significant they were in the creation of poverty-stricken ghettoes and a vast underclass of black proletarians—that massive population at the very bottom of the social class ladder plagued by poor education and low-paying, unstable jobs—they do not provide a meaningful explanation of the life chances of black Americans today. The traditional patterns of interaction between blacks and whites, particularly in the labor market, have been fundamentally altered.

In the antebellum period, and in the latter half of the nineteenth century through the first half of the twentieth century, the continuous and explicit efforts of whites to construct racial barriers profoundly affected the lives of black Americans. Racial oppression was deliberate, overt, and is easily documented, ranging from slavery to segregation, from the endeavors of the white economic elite to exploit black labor to the actions of the white masses to eliminate or neutralize black competition, particularly economic competition.[1] As the nation has entered the latter half of the twentieth century, however, many of the traditional barriers have crumbled under the weight of the political, social, and economic changes of the civil rights era. A new set of obstacles has emerged from basic structural shifts in the economy. These obstacles are therefore impersonal but may prove to be even more formidable for certain segments of the black population. Specifically, whereas the previous barriers were usually designed to control and restrict the entire black population, the new barriers create hardships essentially for the black underclass; whereas the old barriers were based explicitly on racial motivations derived from intergroup contact, the new barriers have racial significance only in their consequences, not in their origins. In short, whereas the old barriers bore the pervasive features of racial oppression, the new barriers indicate an important and emerging form of class subordination.

It would be shortsighted to view the traditional forms of racial segregation and discrimination as having essentially disappeared in contemporary America; the presence of blacks is still firmly resisted in various institutions and social arrangements, for example, residential areas and private social clubs. However, in the economic sphere, class has become more important than race in determining black access to privilege and power. It is clearly evident in this connection that many talented and educated blacks are now entering positions of prestige and influence at a rate comparable to or, in some situations, exceeding that of whites with equivalent qualifications. It is equally clear that the black underclass is in a hopeless state of economic stagnation, falling further and further behind the rest of society.

These brief comments only serve to introduce a problem that is explored in greater detail in the rest of this book as I endeavor to interpret and explain the basis of racial change in America from a macrosociological perspective. The outlines of this perspective are presented in the remaining sections of this chapter, and they provide an analytical framework for examining the shifting areas of racial conflict and the changing experiences of American blacks.

Three Stages of American Race Relations

My basic thesis is that American society has experienced three major stages of black-white contact and that each stage embodies a different form of racial stratification structured by the particular arrangement of both the economy and the polity. Stage one coincides with antebellum slavery and the early postbellum era and may be designated the period of *plantation economy and racial-caste oppression*. Stage two begins in the last quarter of the nineteenth century and ends at roughly the New Deal era and may be identified as the period of *industrial expansion, class conflict, and racial oppression.* Finally, stage three is associated with the modern, industrial, post–World War II era, which really began to crystallize during the 1960s and 1970s, and may be characterized as the period of *progressive transition from racial inequalities to class inequalities.* For the sake of brevity I shall identify the different periods respectively as the preindustrial, industrial, and modern industrial stages of American race relations.

Although this abbreviated designation of the periods of American race relations seems to relate racial change to fundamental economic changes rather directly, it bears repeating that the different stages of race relations are structured by the unique arrangements and interactions of the economy and the polity. Although I stress the economic basis of structured racial inequality in the preindustrial and industrial periods of race relations, I also attempt to show how the polity more or less interacted with the economy either to reinforce patterns of racial stratification or to mediate various forms of racial conflict. Moreover, for the modern industrial period, I try to show how race relations have been shaped as much by important economic changes as by important political changes. Indeed, it would not be possible to understand fully the subtle and manifest changes in race relations in the modern industrial period without recognizing the dual and often reciprocal influence of structural changes in the economy and political changes in the state. Thus, my central argument is that different systems of production and/or different arrangements of the polity have imposed different constraints on the way in which racial groups have interacted in the United States, constraints that have structured the relations between racial groups and that have produced dissimilar contexts not only for the manifestation of racial antagonisms but also for racial group access to rewards and privileges.

In contrast to the modern industrial period in which fundamental economic and political changes have made economic class affiliation more important than race in determining Negro prospects for occupational advancement, the preindustrial and industrial periods of black-white relations have one central feature in common, namely, overt efforts of whites to solidify economic racial domination (ranging from the manipulation of black labor to the neutralization or elimination of black economic competition) through various forms of juridical, political, and social discrimination. Since racial problems during these two periods were principally related to group struggles over economic resources, they readily lend themselves to the economic class theories of racial antagonisms that associate racial antipathy with class conflict. A brief consideration of these theories, followed by a discussion of their basic weaknesses, will help to raise a number of theoretical issues that will be useful for analyzing the dynamics of racial conflict in the preindustrial and industrial stages of American race relations. However, in a later section of this chapter I shall attempt to explain why these theories are not very relevant to the modern industrial stage of American race relations.

Economic Class Theories

Students of race relations have paid considerable attention to the economic basis of racial antagonism in recent years, particularly to the theme that racial problems in historical situations are related to the more general problems of economic class conflict. A common assumption of this theme is that racial conflict is merely a special manifestation of class conflict. Accordingly, ideologies of racism, racial prejudices, institutionalized discrimination, segregation, and other factors that reinforce or embody racial stratification are seen as simply part of a superstructure determined and shaped by the particular arrangement of the class structure.[2] However, given this basic assumption, which continues to be the most representative and widely used economic class argument,[3] proponents have advanced two major and somewhat divergent explanations of how class conflicts actually shape and determine racial relations—the orthodox Marxist theory of capitalist exploitation,[4] and the *split labor-market theory* of working class antagonisms.[5]

The orthodox Marxist theory, which is the most popular variant of the Marxists' explanations of race,[6] postulates that because the ultimate goal of the capitalist class is to maximize profits, efforts will be made to suppress workers' demands for increased wages and to weaken their bargaining power by promoting divisions within their ranks. The divisions occur along racial lines to the extent that the capitalist class is able to isolate the lower-priced black labor force by not only supporting job, housing, and educational discrimination against blacks, but also by developing or encouraging racial prejudices and ideologies of racial subjugation such as racism. The net effect of such a policy is to insure a marginal working class of blacks and to establish a relatively more privileged position for the established white labor force. Since discrimination guarantees a situation where the average wage rate of the black labor force is less than the average wage rate of the established white labor force, the probability of labor solidarity against the capitalist class is diminished.

At the same time, orthodox Marxists argue, the members of the capitalist class benefit not only because they have created a reserved army of labor that is not united against them and the appropriation of surplus from the black labor force is greater than the exploitation rate of the white labor force,[7] but also because they can counteract ambitious claims of the white labor force for higher wages either by threatening to increase the average wage rate of black workers or by replacing segments of the white labor force with segments of the black labor force in special situations such as strikes. The weaker the national labor force, the more likely it is that it will be replaced by lower-paid black labor especially during organized strikes demanding wage increases and improved working conditions. In short, orthodox Marxists argue that racial antagonism is designed to be a "mask for privilege" that effectively conceals the efforts of the ruling class to exploit subordinate minority groups and divide the working class.

In interesting contrast to the orthodox Marxist approach, the split labor-market theory posits the view that rather than attempting to protect a segment of the laboring class, business "supports a liberal or *laissez faire* ideology that would permit all workers to compete freely in an open market. Such open competition would displace higher paid labor. Only under duress does business yield to a labor aristocracy [i.e., a privileged position for white workers]."[8]

The central hypothesis of the split labor-market theory is that racial antagonism first develops in a labor market split along racial lines. The term "antagonism" includes all aspects of intergroup conflict, from beliefs and ideologies (e.g., racism), to overt behavior (e.g., discrimination), to institutions (e.g., segregationist laws). A split labor market occurs when the price of labor for the same work differs for at least two groups, or would differ if they performed the same work. The price of labor "refers to labor's total cost to the employer, including not only wages, but the cost of recruitment, transportation, room and board, education, health care (if the employer must bear these), and the cost of labor unrest."[9]

There are three distinct classes in a split labor market: (1) business or employers; (2) higher-paid labor; and (3) cheaper labor. Conflict develops between these three classes because of different interests. The main goal of business or employers is to maintain as cheap a labor force as possible in order to compete effectively with other businesses and to maximize economic returns. Employers will often import laborers from other areas if local labor costs are too high or if there is a labor shortage. Whenever a labor shortage exists, higher-paid labor is in a good bargaining position. Accordingly, if business is able to attract cheaper labor to the market place, the interests of higher-paid labor are threatened. They may lose some of the privileges they enjoy, they may lose their bargaining power, and they may even lose their jobs. Moreover, the presence of cheaper labor in a particular job market may not only represent actual competition but potential competition as well. An "insignificant trickle" could be seen as the beginning of a major immigration. If the labor market is split along ethnic lines, for example, if higher-paid labor is white and lower-paid labor is black, class antagonisms are transformed into racial antagonisms. Thus, "while much rhetoric of ethnic antagonism concentrates on ethnicity and race, it really in large measure (though probably not entirely) expresses this class conflict."[10]

In some cases members of the lower-paid laboring class, either from within the territorial boundaries of a given country or from another country, are drawn into or motivated to enter a labor market because they feel they can improve their standard of living. As Edna Bonacich points out, "the poorer the economy of the recruits, the less the inducement needed for them to enter the new labor market."[11] In other cases, individuals are forced into a new labor-market situation, such as the involuntary migration of blacks into a condition of slavery in the United States. In this connection, the greater the employer's control over lower-priced labor, the more threatening is lower-paid labor to higher-paid labor.

However, if more expensive labor is strong enough, that is, if it possesses the power resources to preserve its economic interests, it can prevent being replaced or undercut by cheaper labor. On the one hand it can exclude lower-paid labor from a given territory. "Exclusion movements clearly serve the interests of higher paid labor. Its standards are protected, while the capitalist class is deprived of cheaper labor."[12] On the other hand, if it is not possible for higher-paid labor to rely on exclusion (cheaper labor may be indigenous to the territory or may have been imported early in business-labor relations when higher-paid labor could not prevent the move) then it will institutionalize a system of ethnic stratification which could (1) monopolize skilled positions, thereby ensuring the effectiveness of strike action; (2) prevent cheaper labor from developing the skills necessary to compete with higher-paid labor (for example, by imposing barriers to equal access to education); and (3) deny cheaper labor the political resources that would enable them to undercut higher-paid labor through, say, governmental regulations. "In other words, the solution to the devastating potential of weak, cheap labor is, paradoxically, to weaken them further, until it is no longer in business' immediate interest to use them as replacement."[13] Thus, whereas orthodox Marxist arguments associate the development and institutionalization of racial stratification with the motivations and activities of the capitalist class, the split labor-market theory traces racial stratification directly to the powerful, higher-paid working class.

Implicit in both of these economic class theories is a power-conflict thesis associating the regulation of labor or wages with properties (ownership of land or capital, monopolization of skilled positions) that determine the scope and degree of a group's ability to influence behavior in the labor market. Further-more, both theories clearly demonstrate the need to focus on the different ways and situations in which various segments of the dominant racial group perceive and respond to the subordi-nate racial group. However, as I examine the historical stages of race relations in the United States, I find that the patterns of black/white interaction do not consistently and sometimes do not conveniently conform to the propositions outlined in these explanations of racial antagonism. In some cases, the orthodox Marxian explanation seems more appropriate; in other instances, the split labor-market theory seems more appropriate; and in still others, neither theory can, in isolation, adequately explain black-white conflict.

If we restrict our attention for the moment to the struggle over economic resources, then the general pattern that seems to have characterized race relations in the United States during the pre-industrial and industrial stages was that the economic elite seg-ments of the white population have been principally responsible for those forms of racial inequality that entail the exploitation of labor (as in slavery), whereas whites in the lower strata have been largely responsible for those forms of imposed racial stratification that are designed to eliminate economic competition (as in job segregation). Moreover, in some situations, the capitalist class and white workers form an alliance to keep blacks suppressed. Ac-cordingly, restrictive arguments to the effect that racial stratifica-tion was the work of the capitalist class or was due to the "vic-tory" of higher-paid white labor obscure the dyamics of complex and variable patterns of black-white interaction.

However, if we ignore the more categorical assertions that attribute responsibility for racial stratification to a particular class and focus seriously on the analyses of interracial contact in the labor market, then I will be able to demonstrate that, depending on the historical situation, each of the economic class theories provides arguments that help to illuminate race relations during the preindustrial and industrial periods of black-white contact. By the same token, I hope to explain why these theories have little application to the third, and present, stage of modern in-dustrial race relations. My basic argument is that the meaningful

application of the arguments in each theory for any given historical period depends considerably on knowledge of the constraints
imposed by the particular systems of production and by the particular laws and policies of the state during that period, constraints
that shape the structural relations between racial and class groups
and which thereby produce different patterns of intergroup interaction. But first there is another important matter that should
be considered in an analysis of the preindustrial and industrial
stages of American race relations—the interaction between systems of production and racial belief systems.

Industrialization and Racial Belief Systems

When I speak of racial belief systems, I am referring to the norms
or ideologies of racial domination that reinforce or regulate patterns of racial inequality. During the first two stages of American
race relations racial belief systems were quite explicitly based on
assumptions of the black man's biological and cultural inferiority,
and, therefore, have been appropriately identified as ideologies
of racism.[14] The influence of racist norms on intergroup interaction both in and outside of industries has been dismissed as
peripheral by the economic class theorists who tend to relegate
racial belief systems to the ranks of the superstructure. However,
as John Rex appropriately notes, "once a deterministic belief system is used to justify a particular stratification situation, that situation is itself changed thereby and the belief system may set in
motion wholly new social processes."[15] In this connection, Herbert Blumer's discussion of industrialization and race relations,
which relates specifically to the first two stages of American race
relations, provides an interesting contrast to theories that play
down the importance of racial belief systems.[16]

In questioning the conventional assumptions regarding the
rational imperatives of industrialization, Blumer argues that, at
least in the early phases of the growth of industry, business may
be compelled to adhere to the racial norm of exclusion rather
than to depart from it. According to the conventional thesis, a
society undergoing industrialization will be guided by secular
economic interests that place a premium on rational decisions,

undermine the importance attached to traditional racial affiliations, and encourage individual merit and aptitude as the basis of social mobility. "The net import of this conventional view," states Blumer, "is that industrialisation introduces a transitional stage into race relations—a stage marked by unfamiliar association, competitive contact, and a challenge to previous racial standing. Race relations become uncertain and instable. The shifts in them awaken suspicion, arouse resentment, occasion strain and provoke discord."[17] However, Blumer argues that the available evidence illustrates a different pattern in established racial orders. Specifically, employers will tend not to promote or hire minority workers because they are fearful of a possible backlash from dominant-group workers that could disrupt efficient operation. In other words, deeply entrenched societal norms of racial subordination will limit the possibilities for minority social mobility in the labor market. Racial minorities will find ceilings imposed on their occupational advancement that deny their entry into skilled positions and limit their options to only the most poorly paid and menial jobs. Thus, despite the change from status relations in preindustrial societies to contractual relations in industrialized societies, and despite the increased possibilities for upward mobility due to the proliferation of new occupations, the respective positions of racial groups will undergo very little change vis-à-vis the labor market. According to Blumer, "while industrialisation may have disruptive effects at certain points, it may be held in check at other points, and above all may be made to accommodate and fit inside of the traditional order at many other points."[18] In other words, far from producing a breakdown in the traditional racial order, emerging industries merely adapt or adhere to the prevailing racial norms. Subordinate racial members are either restricted to certain jobs or altogether prevented from working in certain industries. Competition between racial groups is therefore limited and racial tensions are held in check. If industrialization does produce racial tensions, this is likely to occur in a society (a) where two groups come together whose relationships have not been previously defined; or (b) where the racial order is definitely disintegrating, usually because of nonindustrial influences, that is, social and political influences.

For Blumer, an established racial order not only connotes a prolonged period of interaction between specific racial groups in a society in which inequality is institutionalized along racial lines, but the system of inequality is reinforced and directed by entrenched societal racial norms, norms that define and prescribe subordinate positions for designated racial groups.[19]

However, it is difficult to determine clearly the influence and strengths of racial norms, even in established racial orders. The unwillingness of industrial managers to challenge the traditional order in some situations may not be based principally on the strength of racial norms but, as suggested in the theory of the split labor market, on the power of the higher-paid labor force to resist any changes that might undermine their position in the labor force irrespective of issues directly related to racialism. Indeed, there have been numerous situations in traditional racial orders where, in order to protect their economic interests, managers took steps that conflicted with prevailing racial norms. For example, industrial management in the northern United States during the second decade of the twentieth century, faced with production demands and an extreme labor shortage created by the curtailment of immigration from Eastern Europe and the heavy induction of white males into the armed services during World War I, deviated from typical racial practices when they openly recruited blacks to work in industries. Prior to this period blacks were ignored, except as occasional strikebreakers, in favor of white immigrant labor. Also in the early twentieth century, South African industrialists took steps to reduce rising costs by allowing blacks to work in certain semiskilled and skilled positions. This change in practice precipitated a serious white workers' strike "on the coal and gold mines which culminated in a general strike on the Witwatersrand leading to the organization of commandos by the strikers, the calling in of troops, the declaration of martial law, and a considerable number of casualties."[20]

There is obviously variation in the way industrial enterprises behave with respect to prevailing racial norms. The evidence suggests that industries tend to conform to racial practices in established racial orders, but variations from the standard patterns require a consideration of such factors as: (a) the strength or saliency of norms of racial exclusion (the greater the role played by these norms in directing and prescribing racial behavior, the less likely they will be challenged; (b) the losses industries will incur in particular situations, for example, if an extreme labor shortage exists, by adhering to the racial norms (the greater the economic losses accompanying conformity to racial norms, the more likely that industrialists will challenge the norms); and (c) the power of the dominant-group workers (the greater the ability of dominant-group workers to protect their economic interests, for example, by generating effective labor strikes or disrupting efficient operation, the less likely that industries will hire minority workers to positions to which dominant-group workers have "prior claim").

Thus, an explanation of the impact of industrialization on race relations should consider the interaction between racial norms, management interests, and workers' power resources. Most certainly, from the vantage point of dominant-group laborers, if labor conflict is associated with management's breaking precedent in allowing certain minority groups to move from their traditional subordinate jobs to positions "reserved" for dominant-group workers, the latter's resistance could be facilitated and strengthened by prevailing racial norms that directly or indirectly justify the opposition to racial realignment. However, as American racial history so clearly reveals, racial norms tend to change as the structural relations between racial groups change. And the main sources of this variation have been the alteration of the system of production and changing policies of the state.

The Influence of the System of Production

The term "system of production" not only refers to the technological basis of economic processes or, in Karl Marx's terms, the "forces of production," but it also implies the "social relations of production," that is, "the interaction (for example, through employment and property arrangement) into which men enter at a given level of the development of the forces of production."[21] As I previously indicated, different systems of production impose constraints on racial group interaction. In the remainder of this section I should like to provide a firmer analytical basis for this distinction as it applies specifically to the three stages of American race relations, incorporating in my discussion relevant theoretical points raised in the foregoing sections of this chapter.

It has repeatedly been the case that a nonmanufacturing or plantation economy with a simple division of labor and a small aristocracy that dominates the economic and political life of a society has characteristically generated a paternalistic rather than a competitive form of race relations, and the antebellum South was no exception.[22] Paternalistic racial patterns reveal close symbiotic relationships marked by dominance and subservience, great social distance and little physical distance, and clearly symbolized rituals of racial etiquette. The southern white aristocracy created a split labor market along racial lines by enslaving blacks to perform tasks at a cheaper cost than free laborers of the dominant group. This preindustrial form of race relations was not based on the actions of dominant-group laborers, who, as we shall see, were relatively powerless to effect significant change in race relations during this period, but on the structure of the relations established by the aristocracy. Let me briefly amplify this point.

In the southern plantation economy, public power was overwhelmingly concentrated in the hands of the white aristocracy. This power was not only reflected in the control of economic resources and in the development of a juridical system that expressed the class interests of the aristocracy, but also in the way the aristocracy was able to impose its viewpoint on the larger society.[23] This is not to suggest that these aspects of public power have not been disproportionately controlled by the economic elite in modern industrialized Western societies; rather it indicates that the hegemony of the southern ruling elite was much greater in degree, not in kind, than in these societies. The southern elite's hegemony was embodied in an economy that required little horizontal or vertical mobility. Further, because of the absence of those gradations of labor power associated with complex divisions of labor, white workers in the antebellum and early postbellum South had little opportunity to challenge the control of the aristocracy. Because white laborers lacked power resources in the southern plantation economy, their influence on the form and quality of racial stratification was minimal through-

out the antebellum and early postbellum periods. Racial stratification therefore primarily reflected the relationships established
between blacks and the white aristocracy, relationships which
were not characterized by competition for scarce resources but
by the exploitation of black labor.[24] Social distance tended to be
clearly symbolized by rituals of racial etiquette: gestures and
behavior reflecting dominance and subservience. Consequently,
any effort to impose a system of public segregation was super-
fluous. Furthermore, since the social gap between the aristocracy
and black slaves was wide and stable, ideologies of racism played
less of a role in the subordination of blacks than they subsequently did in the more competitive systems of race relations
following the Civil War. In short, the relationship represented
intergroup paternalism because it allowed for "close symbiosis
and even intimacy, without any threat to status inequalities."[25]
This was in sharp contrast to the more competitive forms of race
relations that accompanied the development of industrial capitalism in the late nineteenth century and first few decades of the
twentieth century (the industrial period of American race relations), wherein the complex division of labor and opportunities
for greater mobility not only produced interaction, competition,
and labor-market conflict between blacks and the white working
class, but also provided the latter with superior resources (relative to those they possessed under the plantation economy) to
exert greater influence on the form and content of racial stratification.

The importance of the system of production in understanding
race relations is seen in a comparison of Brazil and the southern
United States during the postslavery periods. In the United States,
the southern economy experienced a fairly rapid rate of expansion during the late nineteenth century, thereby creating various
middle level skilled and unskilled positions that working-class
whites attempted to monopolize for themselves. The efforts of
white workers to eliminate black competition in the south generated an elaborate system of Jim Crow segregation that was reinforced by an ideology of biological racism. The white working
class was aided not only by its numerical size, but also by its increasing accumulation of political resources that accompanied
changes in its relation to the means of production.

As white workers gradually translated their increasing labor power into political power, blacks experienced greater restrictions in their efforts to achieve a satisfactory economic, political, and social life. In Brazil, on the other hand, the large Negro and mulatto population was not thrust into competition with the much smaller white population over access to higher-status positions because, as Marvin Harris notes, "there was little opportunity for any member of the lower class to move upward in the social hierarchy."[26] No economic-class group or racial group had much to gain by instituting a rigid system of racial segregation or cultivating an ideology of racial inferiority. Racial distinctions were insignificant to the landed aristocracy, who constituted a numerically small upper class in what was basically a sharply differentiated two-class society originally shaped during slavery. The mulattoes, Negroes, and poor whites were all in the same impoverished lower-ranking position. "The general economic stagnation which has been characteristic of lowland Latin America since the abolition of slavery," observes Marvin Harris, "tends to reinforce the pattern of pacific relationships among the various racial groups in the lower ranking levels of the social hierarchy. Not only were the poor whites outnumbered by the mulattoes and Negroes, but there was little of a significant material nature to struggle over in view of the generally static condition of the economy."[27] Accordingly, in Brazil, segregation, discrimination, and racist ideologies failed to crystallize in the first several decades following the end of slavery. More recently, however, industrialization has pushed Brazil toward a competitive type of race relations, particularly the southern region (for example, São Paulo) which has experienced rapid industrialization and has blacks in economic competition with many lower-status white immigrants.[28]

Whereas the racial antagonism in the United States during the period of industrial race relations (such as the Jim Crow segregation movement in the South and the race riots in northern cities) tended to be either directly or indirectly related to labor-market conflicts, racial antagonism in the period of modern industrial relations tends to originate outside the economic order and to have little connection with labor-market strife. Basic changes in the system of production have produced a segmented labor structure in which blacks are either isolated in the relatively nonunionized, low-paying, basically undesirable jobs of the noncorporate sector, or occupy the higher-paying corporate and government industry positions in which job competition is either controlled by powerful unions or is restricted to the highly trained and educated, regardless of race. If there is a basis for labor-market conflict in the modern industrial period, it is most probably related to the affirmative action programs originating from the civil rights legislation of the 1960s. However, since affirmative action programs are designed to improve job opportunities for the talented and educated, their major impact has been in the higher-paying jobs of the expanding government sector and the corporate sector. The sharp increase of the more privileged blacks in these industries has been facilitated by the combination of affirmative action and rapid industry growth. Indeed despite the effectiveness of affirmative action programs the very expansion of these sectors of the economy has kept racial friction over higher-paying corporate and government jobs to a minimum.

Unlike the occupational success achieved by the more talented and educated blacks, those in the black underclass find themselves locked in the low-paying and dead-end jobs of the noncorporate industries, jobs which are not in high demand and which therefore do not generate racial competition or strife among the national black and white labor force. Many of these jobs go unfilled, and employers often have to turn to cheap labor from Mexico and Puerto Rico. As Nathan Glazer has pointed out, "Expectations have changed, and fewer blacks and whites today will accept a life at menial labor with no hope for advancement, as their fathers and older brothers did and as European immigrants did."[29]

Thus in the modern industrial era neither the corporate or government sectors nor the noncorporate low-wage sector provide the basis for the kind of interracial competition and conflict that has traditionally plagued the labor market in the United States. This, then, is the basis for my earlier contention that the economic class theories which associate labor-market conflicts with racial antagonism have little application to the present period of modern industrial race relations.

The Polity and American Race Relations

If the patterned ways in which racial groups have interacted historically have been shaped in major measure by different systems of production, they have also been undeniably influenced by the changing policies and laws of the state. For analytical purposes, it would be a mistake to treat the influences of the polity and the economy as if they were separate and unrelated. The legal and political systems in the antebellum South were effectively used as instruments of the slaveholding elite to strengthen and legitimate the institution of slavery. But as industrialization altered the economic class structure in the postbellum South, the organizing power and political consciousness of the white lower class increased and its members were able to gain enough control of the political and juridical systems to legalize a new system of racial domination, (Jim Crow segregation) that clearly reflected their class interests.

In effect, throughout the preindustrial period of race relations and the greater portion of the industrial period the role of the polity was to legitimate, reinforce, and regulate patterns of racial inequality. However, it would be unwarranted to assume that the relationship between the economic and political aspects of race necessarily implies that the latter is simply a derivative phenomenon based on the more fundamental processes of the former. The increasing intervention, since the mid-twentieth century, of state and federal government agencies in resolving or mediating racial conflicts has convincingly demonstrated the political system's autonomy in handling contemporary racial problems. Instead of merely formalizing existing racial alignments as in previous periods, the political system has, since the initial state and municipal legislation of the 1940s, increasingly created changes leading to the erosion of traditional racial alignments; in other words, instead of reinforcing racial barriers created during the preindustrial and industrial periods, the political system in recent years has tended to promote racial equality.

Thus, in the previous periods the polity was quite clearly an instrument of the white population in suppressing blacks. The government's racial practices varied, as I indicated above, depending on which segment of the white population was able to assert its class interests. However, in the past two decades the interests of the black population have been significantly reflected in the racial policies of the government, and this change is one of the clearest indications that the racial balance of power had been significantly altered. Since the early 1940s the black population has steadily gained political resources and, with the help of sympathetic white allies, has shown an increasing tendency to utilize these resources in promoting or protecting its group interests.

By the mid-twentieth century the black vote had proved to be a major vehicle for political pressure. The black vote not only influenced the outcome of national elections but many congressional, state, and municipal elections as well. Fear of the Negro vote produced enactment of public accommodation and fair employment practices laws in northern and western municipalities and states prior to the passage of federal civil rights legislation in 1964. This political resurgence for black Americans increased their sense of power, raised their expectations, and provided the foundation for the proliferation of demands which shaped the black revolt during the 1960s. But there were other factors that helped to buttress Negro demands and contributed to the developing sense of power and rising expectations, namely, a growing, politically active black middle class following World War II and the emergence of the newly independent African states.

The growth of the black middle class was concurrent with the growth of the black urban population. It was in the urban areas, with their expanding occupational opportunities, that a small but significant number of blacks were able to upgrade their occupations, increase their income, and improve their standard of living. The middle-class segment of an oppressed minority is most likely to participate in a drive for social justice that is disciplined and sustained. In the early phases of the civil rights movement, the black middle class channeled its energies through organizations such as the National Association for the Advancement of Colored People, which emphasized developing political resources and successful litigation through the courts. These developments were paralleled by the attack against traditional racial alignments in other parts of the world. The emerging newly independent African states led the assault. In America, the so-called "leader of the free world," the manifestation of racial tension and violence has been a constant source of embarrassment to national government officials. This sensitivity to world opinion made the national government more vulnerable to pressures of black protest at the very time when blacks had the greatest propensity to protest.

The development of black political resources that made the government more sensitive to Negro demands, the motivation and morale of the growing black middle class that resulted in the political drive for racial equality, and the emergence of the newly independent African states that increased the federal government's vulnerability to civil rights pressures all combined to create a new sense of power among black Americans and to raise their expectations as they prepared to enter the explosive decade of the 1960s. The national government was also aware of this developing sense of power and responded to the pressures of black protest in the 1960s with an unprecedented series of legislative enactments to protect black civil rights.

The problem for blacks today, in terms of government practices, is no longer one of legalized racial inequality. Rather the problem for blacks, especially the black underclass, is that the government is not organized to deal with the new barriers imposed by structural changes in the economy. With the passage of equal employment legislation and the authorization of affirmative action programs the government has helped clear the path for more privileged   blacks, who have the requisite education and training, to enter the mainstream of American occupations. However, such government programs do not confront the impersonal economic barriers confronting members of the black underclass, who have been effectively screened out of the corporate and government industries. And the very attempts of the government to eliminate traditional racial barriers through such programs as affirmative action have had the unintentional effect of contributing to the growing economic class divisions within the black community.

Class Stratification and Changing Black Experiences

The problems of black Americans have always been compounded because of their low position in both the economic order (the average economic class position of blacks as a group) and the social order (the social prestige or honor accorded individual blacks because of their ascribed racial status). It is of course true that the low economic position of blacks has helped to shape the categorical social definitions attached to blacks as a racial group, but it is also true that the more blacks become segmented in terms of economic class position, the more their concerns about the social significance of race will vary.

In the preindustrial period of American race relations there was of course very little variation in the economic class position of blacks. The system of racial caste oppression relegated virtually all blacks to the bottom of the economic class hierarchy. Moreover, the social definitions of racial differences were heavily influenced by the ideology of racism and the doctrine of paternalism, both of which clearly assigned a subordinate status for blacks vis-à-vis whites. Occasionally, a few individual free blacks would emerge and accumulate some wealth or property, but they were the overwhelming exception. Thus the uniformly low economic class position of blacks reinforced and, in the eyes of most whites, substantiated the social definitions that asserted Negroes were culturally and biogenetically inferior to whites. The uniformly low economic class position of blacks also removed the basis for any meaningful distinction between race issues and class issues within the black community.

The development of a black middle class accompanied the change from a preindustrial to an industrial system of production. Still, despite the fact that some blacks were able to upgrade their occupation and increase their education and income, there were severe limits on the areas in which blacks could in fact advance. Throughout most of the industrial period of race relations, the growth of the black middle class occurred because of the expansion of institutions created to serve the needs of a growing urbanized black population. The black doctor, lawyer, teacher, minister, businessman, mortician, excluded from the white community, was able to create a niche in the segregated black community. Although the income levels and life-styles of the black professionals were noticeably and sometimes conspicuously different from those of the black masses, the two groups had one basic thing in common, a racial status contemptuously regarded by most whites in society. If E. Franklin Frazier's analysis of the black bourgeosie is correct, the black professionals throughout the industrial period of American race relations tended to react to their low position in the social order by an ostentatious display of material possessions and a conspicuous effort to disassociate themselves from the black masses.[30]

Still, as long as the members of the black middle class were stigmatized by their racial status; as long as they were denied the social recognition accorded their white counterparts; more concretely, as long as they remained restricted in where they could live, work, socialize, and be educated, race would continue to be a far more salient and important issue in shaping their sense of group position than their economic class position. Indeed, it was the black middle class that provided the leadership and generated the momentum for the civil rights movement during the mid-twentieth century. The influence and interests of this class were clearly reflected in the way the race issues were defined and articulated. Thus, the concept of "freedom" quite clearly implied, in the early stages of the movement, the right to swim in certain swimming pools, to eat in certain restaurants, to attend certain movie theaters, and to have the same voting privileges as whites. These basic concerns were reflected in the 1964 Civil Rights Bill which helped to create the illusion that, when the needs of the black middle class were met, so were the needs of the entire black community.

However, although the civil rights movement initially failed to address the basic needs of the members of the black lower class, it did increase their awareness of racial oppression, heighten their expectations about improving race relations, and increase their impatience with existing racial arrangements. These feelings were dramatically manifested in a series of violent ghetto outbursts that rocked the nation throughout the late 1960s. These outbreaks constituted the most massive and sustained expression of lower-class black dissatisfaction in the nation's history. They also forced the political system to recognize the problems of human survival and de facto segregation in the nation's ghettoes —problems pertaining to unemployment and underemployment, inferior ghetto schools, and deteriorated housing.

However, in the period of modern industrial race relations, it would be difficult indeed to comprehend the plight of inner-city blacks by exclusively focusing on racial discrimination. For in a very real sense, the current problems of lower-class blacks are substantially related to fundamental structural changes in the economy. A history of discrimination and oppression created a huge black underclass, and the technological and economic revolutions have combined to insure it a permanent status.

As the black middle class rides on the wave of political and social changes, benefiting from the growth of employment opportunities in the growing corporate and government sectors of the economy, the black underclass falls behind the larger society in every conceivable respect. The economic and political systems in the United States have demonstrated remarkable flexibility in allowing talented blacks to fill positions of prestige and influence at the same time that these systems have shown persistent rigidity in handling the problems of lower-class blacks. As a result, for the first time in American history class issues can meaningfully compete with race issues in the way blacks develop or maintain a sense of group position.[31]

Conclusion

The foregoing sections of this chapter present an outline and a general analytical basis for the arguments that will be systematically explored in the following chapters. I have tried to show that race relations in American society have been historically characterized by three major stages and that each stage is represented by a unique form of racial interaction which is shaped by the particular arrangement of the economy and the polity. My central argument is that different systems of production and/or different policies of the state have imposed different constraints on the way in which racial groups interact—constraints that have structured the relations between racial groups and produced dissimilar contexts not only for the manifestation of racial antagonisms but also for racial-group access to rewards and privileges. I emphasized in this connection that in the preindustrial and industrial periods of American race relations the systems of production primarily shaped the patterns of racial stratification and the role of the polity was to legitimate, reinforce, or regulate these patterns. In the modern industrial period, however, both the system of production and the polity assume major importance in creating new patterns of race relations and in altering the context of racial strife. Whereas the preindustrial and industrial stages were principally related to group struggles over economic resources as different segments of the white population overtly sought to create and solidify economic racial domination (ranging from the exploitation of black labor in the preindustrial period to the elimination of black competition for jobs in the industrial period) through various forms of political, juridical, and social discrimination; in the modern industrial period fundamental economic and political changes have made economic class position more important than race in determining black chances for occupational mobility. Finally, I have outlined the importance of racial norms or belief systems, especially as they relate to the general problem of race and class conflict in the preindustrial and industrial periods.

My argument that race relations in America have moved from economic racial oppression to a form of class subordination for the less privileged blacks is not meant to suggest that racial conflicts have disappeared or have even been substantially reduced. On the contrary, the basis of such conflicts have shifted from the economic sector to the sociopolitical order and therefore do not play as great a role in determining the life chances of individual black Americans as in the previous periods of overt economic racial oppression. But these are matters to be explored in greater detail in the following chapters.

2 SLAVERY AND PLANTATION HEGEMONY

In the preindustrial period of American race relations, the system of slavery severely restricted black vertical and horizontal mobility. The basic contacts between blacks and whites were essentially those involving the slaves and the small elite class of slaveowners—a relationship that was stabilized and reinforced by the vast discrepancy in racial power resources on the rural farms and plantations. Being symbiotic in nature, these contacts greatly decreased physical distance; however, social distance was enhanced by clearly defined patterns of dominance and subservience which included elaborate rituals of racial etiquette. There were some slight variations to these patterns both in antebellum southern cities and in relationships involving a small number of free blacks and lower-class whites; but because of the interdependent master-slave relationship, the overwhelming number of blacks in the antebellum South experienced only casual contacts with white nonslaveholders. As the institution of slavery grew, it profoundly affected the pattern of life in the South and, to some extent, in the nation generally. One of slavery's most direct and obvious institutional effects was that it provided the base for the enormous accumulation of public power by a small elite, power that was used to shape the economic structure of the South and the political structure of the nation.

The Hegemony of Southern Slaveholders

Throughout the period of legal servitude, the ownership of slaves was a privilege enjoyed by only a small percentage of free families in the South. Of the 1,156,000 free southern families in 1860, only 385,000 (roughly one-fourth) owned slaves. However, the majority of slaves were owned by families that possessed at least twenty slaves each. Within this "planter class," some ten thousand families, or the "planter aristocracy," owned more than fifty slaves each. The essential point is that, although the great majority of slaveholders owned small farms where a few slaves labored beside their masters, most slaves lived and worked on

plantations where cotton, tobacco, sugar cane, or rice were cultivated on a large, commercial scale.[1]

Despite the fact that power, leadership, and influence were
concentrated among members of the planter class, slaveholders
in general constituted a broad socioeconomic class sharply differentiated from nonslaveholders by social and political behavior
and by basic economic interests. "The most advanced fraction of
the slaveholders—those who most clearly perceived the interests
and needs of the class as a whole," states Genovese, "steadily
worked to make their class more conscious of its nature, spirit,
and destiny. In the process, it created a world-view appropriate
to a slaveholder's regime."[2] By the end of the eighteenth century,
the southern slaveholders had clearly established their hegemony as a regional ruling class. The economic system, the political system, and the juridical system in the South were all controlled and shaped by the slaveholding elite. As a socioeconomic
class, the slaveholders "used their political power to protect
their class interests, the greatest of which was slavery itself."[3]
They also shaped the legal system to reinforce these interests.

The southern legal system embodied an implicit duality that
recognized the rights of the state over both slave and free individuals on the one hand, and the rights of the masters over
their bondsmen on the other. In early Virginia and Maryland, and
later in other colonies, as slavery gradually received legal sanc-
tion, the laws not only granted masters overwhelming power over
their slaves but also codified white supremacy by restricting slave
status to nonwhites and prohibiting interracial marriage. In the
words of Genovese, "These early Draconian slave codes served
as a model for those adopted by new states during the nineteenth
century. Over time, they became harsher with respect to manumission, education, and the status of the free Negro and milder
with respect to protection for slave life."[4]

Although the legal system helped to enhance the interests of
the slaveholders on a regional level, the political system transcended the southern borders and reflected the national influence
of the planters. That the slaveholders were highly organized and
politically disciplined is evident in the way they protected and
promoted their class interests by virtually denying the meaningful exercise of political power to nonslaveholding whites in the

South. At the very least, by the nineteenth century, the procedures used to restrict political participation indicated that the
slaveholders had been transformed, in the classical Marxist dic-
tum, from a class-in-itself to a class-for-itself. "Tradition, property
qualifications for the suffrage, the counting of the slave population
for purposes of legislative apportionment, the gerrymandering of
legislative districts, to the detriment of poor whites, or as in
South Carolina, qualifications which barred office to all but slaveholders," observe Spero and Harris, "made it easy for the master
class to control the state and block all unfavorable legislation."[5]
And this domination of regional politics provided the foundation
for the slaveholders' heavy influence on the federal government
in the latter stages of the antebellum period.

In the first half of the nineteenth century, northern opponents
of slavery contended, with convincing documentation, that the
planters of the South constituted a politically organized "slave
power" that was attempting to control the federal government in
hope of providing more national support for the institution of
slavery. Antislavery Republicans of the North did not hesitate to
point out that since 1789 a substantial majority of congressional
committee chairmen, chief justices, secretaries of state, and even
presidents had been from the South.[6] In 1856, the *New York
Times*, echoing the sentiments of antislavery men, editorialized
that the southern politicians were "held together like the feudal
barons of the middle ages by a community of interests and of
sentiment; and [act] together always for the promotion of their
common ends."[7]

The southerners' power in Congress and in the electoral college had been increased by the three-fifths clause of the Constitution to the point where they could regulate the policies of the
major parties on slavery. Meanwhile, northern sentiment was
weakened by fear of southern threats of secession and by a lack
of unity on the issue of slavery. A succession of congressional
decisions in the decades preceding the Civil War served to dram-
atize the influence of the planter class on the Federal government and lent strong support to the idea of "slave power." Sal-
mon P. Chase, the influential antislavery leader of Ohio, pointed
out in 1854 that the eighteenth-century policy of restricting and
denationalizing slavery was seriously undermined when a report
dealing with slavery was altered by the very first Congress to

satisfy slaveholders' interests, when the fugitive slave law was passed, and when Congress accepted a territorial cession from North Carolina which allowed slavery to exist in the area. He furthermore noted that the creation of slavery and slaveholdings in areas of national jurisdiction continued into the nineteenth century; Florida and Louisiana were purchased with slavery permitted, the Missouri Compromise extended slavery across the Mississippi River, and the annexation of Texas increased slave power in the Southwest.[8] The Kansas-Nebraska Act of 1854, which dramatically opened the West to slavery, and the Dred-Scott Decision of 1857, which provided federal government protection of slavery in the territories, extended southern influence in the federal government and clearly demonstrated the reality of an aggressive slave power.

The hegemony of the southern slaveholders as a regional ruling class and their influence on national politics emanated directly from a slave-based plantation economy which impeded the ability of nonslaveholders to challenge the planters' political and economic stranglehold over the South; it also enabled the slaveholders to develop a regional center of power that was effectively transferred to the national level. As long as the replenishing of the labor supply did not depend on tapping the reservoir of free labor, slavery as a mode of production created a situation in which economic power was consolidated and concentrated in the hands of the slaveholding elite. With slaves providing the bulk of the labor for the plantations and, as we shall see, a good share of the meager industrial labor force, the competitive advantage of free laborers in an essentially preindustrial economy was drastically curtailed. The weak economic position of nonslaveholding whites provided little leverage for generating social and political power and for developing a sufficient political class consciousness. These whites were not even in a position to exert much influence on the pattern of race relations in the antebellum South.

Structural Relations between Masters and Slaves

There are two distinct historical periods marking the relationship between masters and slaves—the period prior to the cessation of the African slave trade in 1808 in which the planters relied partly on external markets for the reproduction of their labor force and the period following the ban on slave trading in which the reproduction of slave labor was based almost exclusively on natural increase. The significance of this distinction is that many historians feel that the treatment of slaves was considerably harsher in the period prior to the United States' official withdrawal from the African slave trade; there was harsher treatment, it is said, primarily because planters were not compelled to devote serious attention to slave reproduction. However, the issues underlying this assumption are fairly complex and deserve at least a brief discussion on the basis of the available, but far from satisfactory, evidence.

Despite the heightened interest in scholarly interpretations of American slavery and the slave experience (generated in large measure by the controversial studies of Stanley Elkins, Eugene Genovese, and Robert Fogel and Stanley Engerman),[9] recent historical debates on the subject have tended to focus more on nineteenth-century slavery (that is, the period following the ban on slave trading) than on the earlier periods. However, an important study by Edmund S. Morgan on slavery in Virginia has helped to fill some of the gaps in our knowledge about the peculiar institution in the colonial period.[10]

If we examine the situation in colonial Virginia (the first colony to officially recognize slavery, with an act passed in 1661 that made an indentured servant who ran away with a slave responsible for the loss incurred by the master during the slave's absence) around the mid-seventeenth century, we see that the conversion to slavery was not only prompted by the heightened concern over a cheap labor shortage in the face of the rapid development of tobacco farming as a commercial enterprise and the declining number of white indentured servants entering the colonies,[11] but also by the fact that the slave had become a better investment than the servant. As life expectancy increased, resulting from the significant decline in the mortality rate from disease, planters were willing to finance the extra cost of slaves. Indeed, during the first half of the seventeenth century, indentured labor was actually more advantageous than slave labor. "Because of the high mortality among the immigrants to Virginia," states Morgan, "there could be no great advantage in owning a man for lifetime rather than a period of years, especially since a slave cost roughly twice as much as an indentured servant. If the chances of a man's dying during his first five years in Virginia were better than fifty-fifty—and it seems apparent that they were—and if English servants could be made to work as hard as slaves, English servants for a five year term were the better buy."[12]

Because the international slave trade had already firmly established a pattern of black enslavement and because there was no deep-seated opposition to the institution of slavery in the colonies, the increased life expectancy during the second half of the seventeenth century just made it a matter of time before slavery would replace indentured servitude as a major source of cheap labor. It was not necessary to enslave anyone to establish slavery in Virginia: "Virginians had only to buy men who were already enslaved, after the initial risks of the transformation had been sustained by others elsewhere. They converted to slavery, simply by buying slaves instead of servants."[13]

Although slaves in the colonies entered a system of production that had already been established, their presence necessitated new methods of disciplining the work force. In Virginia, for instance, masters of slaves soon recognized the need to impose a higher level of pain than did the masters of servants. "Slaves could not be made to work for fear of losing liberty," observes Morgan, "so they had to be made to work for fear for their lives. Not that any master wanted to lose his slave by killing him, but in order to get an equal or greater amount of work, it was necessary to beat slaves harder than servants, so hard, in fact, that there was a much larger chance of killing them than had been the case with servants."[14] Indeed, the Virginia Assembly recognized this fact and in 1669 passed a law which would legally protect the master who in the process of disciplining his slave actually ended up killing him. Later legislation designed to curb the growing problem of runaway slaves stipulated that it would "be lawful for any person or persons whatsoever, to kill and destroy such slaves by such ways and means as he, she, or they shall think fit, without accusation or impeachment of any crime for the same."[15] The law further specified that the master would be compensated with public funds for the loss of any slaves killed under these conditions. Thus, concludes Morgan, "In order to get work out of men and women who had nothing to gain but the absence of pain, you had to be willing to beat, maim, and kill. And society had to be ready to back you, even to the point of footing the bill for the property you killed."[16]

However, colonial laws which allowed masters and other whites to kill slaves were not extended into the nineteenth century. By 1821, all slave states had amended their laws to protect the lives of slaves and to provide murder indictments against slaveholders and others for killing a slave arbitrarily or through excessive punishment. As Genovese points out in this connection, "When whites did find themselves before the bar of justice, especially during the late antebellum period, they could expect greater severity than might be imagined. The penalties seldom reached the extreme or the level they would have if the victim had been white; but neither did they usually qualify as a slap on the wrist. If one murderer in North Carolina got off with only eleven months in prison in 1825, most fared a good deal worse. Ten-year sentences were common, and occasionally the death penalty was invoked."[17]

It is always a precarious practice to infer the actual treatment of human beings from laws that regulate human behavior. However, a comparison of the laws pertaining to the killing of slaves in the colonial period with the more humane laws in the nineteenth century does suggest a change in societal norms regarding slavery, even if one is not willing to grant any significant changes in the actual behavior of white slaveholders. Still, there are other indications that the lot of slaves fared better in the late antebellum period than in the colonial period. But, before examining these other factors, I want to return to the argument concerning the significance of the cessation of the African slave trade—an argument that some historians have used to explain changes in the treatment of slaves.

The closing of the slave trade in the early nineteenth century did not weaken the institution of slavery, as some Americans might have expected. Rather, it had a reverse effect. It increased the financial commitment of slavery. Because slaves could no longer be legally imported from Africa and because the demand for slaves sharply increased both with the opening of new lands in the Southwest and with the expanding of cotton production in the deep South, the price of bondsmen skyrocketed in the nineteenth century. Even those slaveholders who resided in areas such as Virginia and South Carolina where slave labor was no longer as important as it had been in the past, became more firmly committed to slavery as their investment in human property increased in value.[18]

In addition to the increased financial commitment to slavery, the slave-trade ban increased the reliance on natural reproduction for replenishing the slave population. It therefore became increasingly important for slaveholders to give attention to the material conditions of slaves in order to improve the chances for successful childbirth and physical growth to maturity.[19] Recent historical studies by Fogel and Engerman and by Genovese have asserted that the treatment of slaves progressively improved throughout the nineteenth century and that the rapid natural growth of slavery was associated with more humane treatment.[20] Following federal action in 1808, declaring the importation of slaves illegal, the slave population grew, primarily as a result of natural increase, from one million in 1810 to nearly four million in 1860.[21] The South's experience of rapid slave population growth via natural increase was unique. Despite significantly larger importations throughout the eighteenth and nineteenth centuries, Cuba, Brazil, Jamaica, and Santo Domingo struggled simply to maintain their slave populations by balancing imports against mortality.[22] Fogel and Engerman maintain that the slaveholders in the South provided slaves with material conditions that "compared favorably with those of free industrial workers during the first half of the nineteenth century,"[23] including a diet which "actually exceeded modern (1964) recommended daily levels of chief nutrients."[24] Genovese likewise stresses that the slaves were as well off as a substantial portion of Western European peasants and workers and that the slaveholders during this same period came to fully realize that excessive driving jeopardized the slaves' health and, therefore, contributed to capital loss. "They even enlisted racist arguments to advocate a more humane course, explaining that blacks constitutionally could not work as long as whites."[25]

Both the improved treatment of slaves and their rapid natural growth were, however, a function of the increasing value of slave property in the nineteenth century. To repeat, the price of slaves escalated in the face of expanding cotton production in the deep South and the demand for labor in the newly settled territories of the Southwest. It is little wonder, therefore, that the southern slave system "became progressively more humane with respect to the material conditions of life as it became progressively more repressive with respect to manumission."[26] Nearing the eve of the Civil War, slavery had become a very profitable and success- ful institution and the drive to improve the material conditions of slaves as well as the campaign to decrease their chances of freedom, both of which predated abolitionist pressures, derived from the planters' interests in maximizing profits.

The slaveholders often responded to criticisms of their efforts to maintain blacks in permanent bondage by proclaiming not only that their bondsmen were treated better than any other slaves in the world but also that their conditions compared fav- orably with those of the workers and peasants in Europe. Their arguments, of course, selectively focused on the material condi- tions of life. The slaveholders were not inclined to consider the psychological aspects of slavery outlined in the eloquent remarks of W. E. B. DuBois in 1934:

> But there was in 1863 a real meaning to slavery different from that we apply to the laborer today. It was in part psychological, the enforced personal feeling of inferiority, the calling of another master, the standing with hat in hand. It was the helplessness. It was the defenselessness of family life. It was the submergence below the arbitrary will of any sort of individual. It was without doubt worse in these vital respects than that which exists today in Europe or America.[27]

Whether one focuses on slavery in the colonial period or in the late antebellum period, "the enforced personal feeling of inferiority" was endemic to permanent servitude. The slave was under constant supervision and efforts were consistently made to generate deferential and submissive behavior. The enduring ritual of race etiquette, reinforced by the master at every turn, stipu- lated that proper behavior and conduct for blacks involved bow- ing when meeting the master, standing and showing great humil- ity in his presence, accepting floggings from the master's children, and approaching the mansion in the most self-effacing, humble, and beseeching manner. Floggings and other modes of physical punishment were employed by most planters to ensure ritualistic obedience and deference to plantation rules. Slaves were frequently flogged, punished, or disciplined for failing to complete assigned tasks, running away, learning to read, bickering or fighting with whites or with other slaves, stealing, drunkenness, working too slowly, impertinence, asking to be sold, claiming their freedom, and damaging tools or household articles.[28]

But were the bondsmen psychologically devastated by slavery? It is one thing to recognize the group or personal feelings of inferiority that are inevitably produced by prolonged enslavement, it is quite another to postulate, as does Stanley Elkins, that slaves, very much like Jews in the Nazi concentration camps, were reduced to a childlike dependency.[29] A series of historical studies have challenged Elkins' thesis by positing the view that the institution of slavery left enough "breathing space" for slaves to develop mechanisms or strategies of survival to preserve their humanity, to resist complete personal degradation, to prevent total identification with masters, and to stave off infantilism.[30] Historians disagree, however, in their interpretation of just how and in what context these mechanisms were developed. And to get an idea of the level of disagreement, we need only examine the arguments advanced by Eugene Genovese and Herbert G. Gutman, whose works provide two of the most important and persuasive theses on slave strategies of survival.[31]

According to Genovese, the efforts of slaves to preserve their humanity grew out of and were in part based on the unique form of paternalism that characterized antebellum slavery in the South. Encouraged by the physical proximity and continuous interaction between planters and slaves, southern paternalism stressed duties, responsibilities, and reciprocal demands and expectations. The ideological expression of southern paternalism not only justified slave labor as a legitimate exchange for the masters' protection and direction but also, by the doctrine of reciprocal obligations, implicitly acknowledged the slaves' humanity. In fact, the slaves seized on this interpretation and translated paternalism into a doctrine that greatly stressed their human rights. If it were the master's duty to care for his involuntary labor force, then this duty represented the slaves' right. The slaves' acceptance of paternalism, therefore, signified acceptance of imposed white control within which they established limits, affirmed their rights, and spared their self-respect.[32] "By developing a sense of moral worth and by asserting their rights, the slaves transformed their acquiescence in paternalism into a rejection of slavery itself, although their masters assumed acquiescence in one to demonstrate acquiescence in the other."[33]

Genovese maintains that it was the slaves' religion, a complex mixture of African and Christian beliefs, that provided the medium for elaborating this interpretation of paternalism, a religion that created an organized center of resistance within accommodation, a religion, in short, that reflected white hegemony but also established definite limits to that hegemony. "Southern paternalism may have reinforced racism as well as class exploitation," argues Genovese, "but it also unwittingly invited its victims to fashion their own interpretation of the social order it was intended to justify. And the slaves, drawing on a religion that was supposed to assure their compliance and docility, rejected the essence of slavery by protecting their rights and values as human beings."[34]

Whereas Genovese believes that slaves developed mechanisms to preserve their humanity based on continuous interaction with or reaction to the behavior of planters, Gutman argues that the bondsmen were far more independent in the development of slave communities. By reconstructing the slave family and kinship structure through a careful analysis of plantation birth registers, marriage applications received by Union officers following emancipation, and documents containing the direct testimony of former slaves, Gutman attempts to show that an adaptive Afro-American slave culture was created without any significant involvement or influence exerted by the planters. Instead of using cultural forms that emerged from a manipulation of planter paternalism, slaves adapted in fairly uniform ways to diversified forms of enslavement (living on plantations or in farm counties, or in counties in which few or many slaves resided) by developing and using social and cultural arrangements that white planters did not even perceive. Specifically, Gutman maintains that enslaved Afro-Americans independently developed distinctive domestic arrangements and kin networks that fostered a new Afro-American culture, and that both the family system and the slave culture provided the social basis for the creation of Afro-American communities. In other words, the development of inter- and intra-generational linkages, following the emergence of settled Afro-American slave families provided a basis for a sense of community that was extended over time and across space. Thus, conceptions of kin and family obligations among slaves were transformed by the slaves themselves into conceptions of quasi-kin and nonkin social and communal obligations. Slaves in this network of social obligations and attachments exhibited neither the "social isolation" described in Elkins' study of slavery nor the "elaborate web of paternalistic relations," that, according to Genovese, allowed the planter class to establish "hegemony over the slaves."[35]

These conflicting interpretations of the slave experience and the master-slave relationship will continue to generate debate among historians until future research sheds additional light on the subject. If blacks were able to develop unique "strategies for survival," whether by a paternalistic compromise or an independent cultural adaptation, they did so in a racial caste system that exploited their labor, restricted their freedom, and virtually eliminated any chances for free and open competition for scarce rewards and privileges. Moreover, regardless of the degree of cultural independence displayed by the slaves, much of their behavior was influenced or determined by their continuous interaction or relationships with slaveholding whites. The very nature of such a relationship (characterized by dominance and subservience, little physical distance but great social distance) would suggest at least a modicum of paternalistic behavior, because, unlike in more competitive systems of race relations, it allowed for close symbiotic relationships without necessarily threatening the norms of racial inequality. Furthermore, as Genovese points out, many of the informal norms of the paternalistic order, norms which stipulated the masters' obligation to care for their slaves in return for explicit duties and services, were actually formalized or embodied in the nineteenth-century slave codes.[36] Finally, even Gutman recognizes that "Paternalist beliefs were wide-spread among plantation owners on the eve of the Civil War and affected the behavior of many planters." However, he is correct in further pointing out that "no one, including Genovese, has studied how such beliefs and practices developed."[37] Since the available evidence suggests that paternalistic beliefs among planters were more characteristic of the nineteenth century than of the seventeenth and eighteenth centuries, it would not be unreasonable to associate those beliefs with the increasing value of slave property after the closing of the African slave trade.

It could even be argued that the tendency of southern blacks to separate Caucasians into the "respectable" and the "poor white trash" in the late nineteenth and the twentieth centuries was one of the legacies of slave paternalism. Slaves were clearly cognizant of the protection that the paternalistic order provided them against overt attacks by hostile poor whites. Even with the sharp increase in the slave population during the late antebellum period, as long as paternalistic relations between masters and slaves existed, the racial antagonisms of the nonslaveholding whites were held in check. Lynching, which typified the informal violence of the antebellum South, seldom involved blacks. Genovese estimates that less than 10 percent of the more than three hundred lynching victims between 1840 and 1860 were black.[38] The masters had little need to engage in or to support extralegal measures against blacks because of their power not only over their slaves but also in the larger society. If indiscriminate mob violence against slaves was tolerated, the position of the slave-holding class would be challenged as well and the aggressive activities of the white lower class might eventually exceed racial boundaries. "The masters felt that their own direct action, buttressed by a legal system of their own construction, needed little or no support from poor white trash. Order meant order."[39]

The slaves' reliance on their masters for protection established a pattern of group dependency that was to persist several decades after slavery officially ended. And, as we shall see in the next chapter, when this relationship ultimately collapsed in the postbellum period, it paved the way for a century of Jim Crow segregation.

Slavery and Segregation in the Antebellum Urban South

Whereas paternalistic relations, reinforced by slaveholder power, tended to characterize black-white relations on the rural farms and plantations, a noticeably different pattern of racial inter- action prevailed in the urban areas of the antebellum South where assertive free blacks, insecure underclass whites, and loosely supervised slaves lived and worked. On the farms and plantations, the social distance between the races was wide and secure. Consequently, the system of status inequalities was not threatened by the high degree of black-white contact and inter- action. In rather sharp contrast to this rural pattern, roles and statuses attached to race were somewhat ambiguous in the cities of the Old South.

The ambiguity was exacerbated by the presence of free blacks, never more than a quarter million, who tended to reside in the cities of the Upper South, but who were not unnoticeable in certain cities in the Lower South. Moreover, urban slavery dif- fered quite significantly from slavery on the rural farms and plan- tations because urban slaves were not as closely supervised and therefore experienced much greater mobility.[40] The increasing complexities and changing needs of the urban economy required a continuous reallocation of labor to accommodate the supply and demand. The imperatives of urban life thus produced a flex- ible system of slave labor, including an arrangement whereby slaves were used not only in the master's home or business but also were hired out to other employers.

The hiring-out system was accomplished in two ways. One involved simply the binding of a slave to another master. This practice was occasionally used in rural areas. The other permitted a slave to work for several masters at different times and oc- curred exclusively in urban areas. Although the hiring-out system provided the flexibility required in the urban economic order, it created problems that ultimately undermined the authority of the slavery institution. As Richard C. Wade has pointed out:

> Soon owners found it easier and usually more profitable to permit their bondsmen to find their own employment. . . . This created a new dimension of independence for the

Negroes, since it circumvented the elaborate controls municipalities had placed around the hiring process. Under this
arrangement, masters told their Negroes to locate a job,
make their own agreement on wages, and simply bring back
a certain sum every week or month. The slave, moreover,
could pocket any profit he made.[41]

The more the slave was permitted to seek his own employment, the further he was removed from close white supervision.
Despite public restrictions designed to prevent blacks from hiring
themselves out, slaves generally had the liberty to choose their
employers and to arrange their own room and board. If a slave
made regular payments to his master and if he was able to avoid
the attention of the police, he experienced a fair degree of
liberty. This was anything but a satisfactory arrangement to nonslaveholders concerned about keeping the black population,
slave and free, under control, and it was particularly disturbing
to the working-class elements fearful of black competition for
jobs.

Prior to the nineteenth century, urban blacks were kept divided
and could not develop cohesive groups in the cities of the South.
This was achieved by white efforts to prevent the emergence of
geographically segregated Negro housing. In every southern city,
"blacks and whites lived side by side, sharing the same premises
if not equal facilities and being constantly in each other's presence."[42] Even the white nonslaveholders found themselves living
near or next to blacks. Slaves who "lived out" and were not
under the direct supervision of their masters could not avoid
whites as neighbors; furthermore, free blacks were scattered
throughout the city.

However, the pressures of urban living gradually altered the
residential patterns of Dixie cities. The housing policy, designed
to prevent black concentration, required the twenty-four-hour
supervision of slave activity. Inevitably, this proved difficult in
the cities where human contact was maximized and where slaves
developed independence by working away from their masters,
by being hired out, by living out, and by mixing openly with free
blacks. In time, small slumlike sections populated by both slaves
and free blacks emerged, usually on the edge of the city.

In the strict sense of the term, "segregation," or separation of the races, had always existed under slavery. In the rural plantation, certain tasks were assigned to slaves, and slave quarters were removed from the masters' quarters, thereby limiting contact during nonworking hours. But racial separation was never a matter of public policy on the rural plantation. The master-servant model clearly established a superordinate-subordinate relationship between whites and blacks, and the manner in which the master handled his slaves in day-to-day discipline was largely a private matter. But, in urban areas, it soon became apparent that the handling of slaves could not be left to the master's discretion. There, spatial relations were significantly different. "Both races were thrown together; they encountered each other at every corner, they rubbed elbows at every turn; they divided up, however inequitably, the limited space of the town site. Segregation sorted people by race, established a public etiquette for their conduct, and created social distance where there was proximity."[43]

But the segregation that existed in the antebellum urban South is significant only to document the effect of different structural relations on the quality and form of race relations. It demonstrates that when paternalistic patterns of the kind manifested in the rural plantations break down, race relations shift to a more competitive pattern. Segregation replaces paternalistic racial etiquette as a symbol of the racial caste barrier and as a form of racial control. Unlike the rural plantation system where the structure of racial inequality is primarily a product of the relationship between the slaveholders and the slaves, in the cities the relationship between blacks, slave and free, and all segments of the white population shaped racial stratification. In the final analysis, however, race relations in the antebellum cities were far from representative of the South. Over 90 percent of the population resided in rural areas by 1860 and was not exposed to public segregation. Despite the fact that the cities had significant influence on southern life, the racial climate below the Mason-Dixon line is more accurately gauged by focusing on the rural rather than on the urban areas. And even in the cities, the pattern of segregation and other manifestations of competitive race relations were never anywhere as harsh or developed as in the postbellum South or even the late antebellum North.

It is true, as discussed above, that urban race relations in the antebellum South were more ambiguous than in the rural areas and that the status of blacks was less clearly defined. But it is also true that the nonslaveholders, the group that had the most to gain by racial segregation, lacked the power or resources to develop the more extensive and pervasive forms of racial separation that would have restricted black employment and more effectively isolated blacks in certain sections of the city. The business class therefore showed little hesitation in tapping the reservoir of cheap black labor for a variety of handicraft and industrial jobs. And the demand for urban slaves, contrary to previous assumptions, actually accelerated as the country approached the eve of the Civil War.[44] Moreover, since the very existence of slavery stigmatized blacks, the pressure to create segregated institutions never reached the heights attained in the period of Jim Crow segregation following the Civil War. In that period, the rise of the white lower class significantly altered the traditional patterns of racial contact in the South. However, one need not turn to the period following the Civil War to gauge the effect of an organized and assertive landless white population on the relationship between blacks and whites. For the kind of racial segregation characteristic of that period had already been demonstrated in the North in the three decades preceding the Civil War. Indeed, in the following chapter, I shall attempt to show that the role of poor whites in shaping racial stratification was as significant in the late antebellum North as in the racially repressive Jim Crow era of the postbellum South.

Conclusion

In this chapter, I have attempted to show how the preindustrial system of production shaped the pattern of race relations in the antebellum South. The hegemony of the slave owners as a regional ruling class derived from a slave-based plantation economy which effectively rendered nonslaveholders powerless and thereby enabled plantation owners to develop almost total control of the political and economic life of the South. The slaveholders' domination of southern politics provided the foundation for their strong influence on national politics regarding the issue of slavery, an influence which ultimately contributed to the growth and stability of the "peculiar institution."

Since nonslaveholding whites were stripped of economic and political power, they had little effect on the patterns of race relations in the antebellum South. And since the meaningful forms of black-white contact were between slaves and the elite class of slaveowners, race relations assumed a pattern in which norms, duties, rights, and obligations (whether in the slave community, or the slaveholder community, or the community of masters and slaves) were all defined and elaborated vis-à-vis the exploitation of black labor. These normative expectations tended to change as the institution of slavery assumed a more clear-cut paternalistic pattern in the late antebellum period, but they continued to reflect the enormous power discrepancy between masters and slaves on the rural plantations and farms.

It is true that in the urban South, where many free blacks were concentrated, a more competitive pattern of race relations emerged that led to the development of segregation as a form of racial control; but, as I attempted to show, such patterns were not representative of the region. In short, the antebellum South displayed a pervasive racial caste system created, institutionalized, and rationalized by the white economic elite. The implications of this system of inequality for the previously discussed economic class theories of racial antagonisms is one of the subjects of the following chapter.

SEGREGATION AND THE RISE OF THE
WHITE WORKING CLASS

A split labor market along racial lines developed early in the history of the United States as a result of the institutionalization of slavery: split in the sense that slave labor was considered cheaper than free white labor. Aside from the fact that, unlike slaves, white laborers could strike and press for increased wages, thereby narrowing the difference between production cost and profit, the planter and business classes believed that in most situations slave labor was simply a less expensive investment. For example, a Louisiana state senate committee for the construction of canals, levees, and plank roads calculated in 1853 that the state would save $79,140 a year if three hundred slave carpenters and mechanics were used in favor of three hundred white laborers. The figures in Table 1 indicate that if slaves were bought at $1,000 a head, the annual savings on slave labor would actually pay for the original cost in less than four years.[1]

Slaves were trained in virtually every branch of skilled and unskilled labor.[2] Those who were not needed on the plantation at a particular time were hired out to firms for construction work and numerous other semiskilled and unskilled jobs.[3] The more frequent the contact between black slaves and white workers in the labor market, the more the wages of white workers were depressed to the level of the price required for the hire of slaves.[4]

Bernard Mandel, in his impressive book *Labor: Free and Slave*, stated that:

> Not only did the laborers have to meet the price of slave labor, but they also had to produce as much as slaves to hold their own in the struggle for existence, and consequently had to deliver a long day's labor. The ten-hour movement never achieved the dimensions that it did in the North, and had little possibility of success in those circumstances. When the journeymen bricklayers of Louisville were struggling for the ten-hour system, they met an insuperable obstacle in the fact that they were replaceable by slaves, so they had to work as many hours as the slaves or abandon their trade. The stonecutters were able to win the ten-hour

day because no slaves were employed in that occupation. But when the carpenters and painters called a strike for shorter hours, it was broken by the employment of slaves on their jobs; some strikers went back to work on the old terms, and others, disgusted and demoralized, emigrated from the state.[5]

Herman Schluter perceived the effect of slavery on white labor in much the same way by observing that, whereas in 1852 the wages of free laborers in the cotton mills of Tennessee barely amounted to 50 cents a day for males and $1.25 a week for females, in Lowell, Massachusetts, the wages were 80 cents a day and $2.00 a week for men and women cotton-mill workers respectively.[6] And Philip Foner informs us that competition with slave labor reduced wages for southern white workers to the lowest in the nation. "The daily wages in 1860 for day laborers in the North was about $1.11, whereas in most southern states it was between 77 and 90 cents. The daily wage for carpenters in the North for the same year was about $2, while in many states in the South it did not exceed $1.56. While operatives in Georgia cotton factories were earning $7.39 a month, workers in textile mills in Massachusetts doing the same work were getting $14.74."[7]

TABLE 1. Annual Net Savings from the Use of Slave Labor over Free Labor

Free Labor	
300 whites, hired at $30 a month, per year	$108,000
Provisions	18,000
6 superintendents, at $1,000	6,000
Total cost of free labor per year	$132,000
Slave Labor	
(300 slaves, bought at $1,000 each	$300,000)
Interest on investment, at 5%	$ 15,000
Provisions and clothes	16,500
Loss of slaves by death, etc.	15,000
6 superintendents, at $1,000	6,000
Extra food for superintendents	360
Total cost of slave labor per year	$ 52,860
Balance in favor of slave labor	$ 79,140

Source: Roger W. Shugg, *Origins of Class Struggle in Louisiana* (Louisiana State University Press, 1939), p. 89.

The threat to hire slaves was used even in industries where they were not employed. White laborers held meetings throughout the South, endorsing resolutions and presenting petitions to state legislatures and city councils describing the disastrous effects of black competition and demanding laws to prohibit the apprenticing of blacks for skilled trades, to restrict the movement of slaves and free blacks seeking jobs, and to exclude slaves and free blacks from mechanical occupations. Among those who protested were: a group of white carpenters in Wilmington, North Carolina, who in 1857 burned a building that had recently been erected by slaves and who threatened to burn all structures built by slaves in the future; a group of unemployed white stonecutters who in 1830 petitioned the Department of the Navy in Washington, D.C., to discontinue using slave labor in the construction of a dry dock for the navy; and a group of white mechanics who petitioned the legislature of Virginia in 1831 to end the competition of slave mechanics.[8] However, except for a few cases where white laborers were successful in getting legislation passed to neutralize both slave and free black competition (in Charleston, South Carolina, legislation was enacted in 1765 restricting the use of free Negroes and slaves as mechanics and handicraft workers, and in Georgia similar legislation was passed in 1758 prohibiting the employment of a black mechanic or mason),[9] laws generated by white workers were confined in their application to free Negroes. The laws wanted most by white laborers—laws to restrict the employment of slaves—were repeatedly defeated in councils and state legislatures because they conflicted with the interests of employers and slaveholders.[10] Organized labor was weak in the face of the overwhelming political and economic resources of the master class. Thus as Schluter has remarked:

> The free white laborer in South Carolina, for instance, could vote, but not for one of his own class; only a slave-owner could be governor; and the Legislature, composed exclusively of slave-owners, appointed the judges, the magistrates, the senators and the electors for President. And as in South Carolina, so approximately in the other states of the South.[11]

On the surface, the class and racial tensions associated with labor market conflicts in the antebellum South seem to correspond with the arguments advanced in the split labor-market theory of worker racial antagonism. The labor market was split along racial lines; the interests of higher-paid white labor were threatened by the employers' wide use of black labor; class conflicts were expressed in racial antagonism. Moreover, in view of the problems slavery created for wage labor, it is not unreasonable to assume that white laborers would have taken steps to prevent the growth of slavery had they the power to do so. The nonslaveholding masses, who constituted three-fourths of all antebellum white southerners, were too politically weak to resist being displaced or undercut by slave labor. All of these facts are consistent with the split labor-market theory.

There is some evidence which challenges aspects of the split labor-market theory and lends support to the orthodox Marxist's explanation of racial antagonism. More specifically, the former's argument that the business class does not purposefully play off one segment of the working class against the other is not upheld when the actions taken by slaveholders to preserve the institution of slavery are examined. Although it is difficult to uphold the Marxist argument that the slaveholders were actually committed to providing a more privileged economic position for white laborers than for slaves, the slaveholders' rhetoric was designed to convince white laborers that they had a vested interest in the preservation of the system of slavery. After reviewing documentary evidence, Mandel concluded that white laborers "were constantly told that, by confining the hard, menial and low-paid tasks to the slaves, the white workers were enabled to constitute a labor aristocracy which held the best and most dignified jobs, and that the latter were lucrative only because they were supported by the superprofits wrung from the unpaid labor of slaves."[12] In response to the abolitionists' argument that slavery was detrimental to both free and slave labor, the slaveholders argued that, if slavery were abolished, "the whites would have to take over the menial jobs and the emancipated slaves would be able to compete with them in every branch of industry."[13]

Furthermore, the rigid racial caste system of slavery was not the creation of higher-paid white labor opposed to black competition but of a handful of powerful plantation owners who hoped to maximize their economic resources through bound, controlled labor. Finally, the planters created and cultivated the ideology of biological racism, declaring blacks biogenetically inferior to whites, both as a weapon to justify the system of slavery when it was under attack from abolitionists in the later eighteenth and early nineteenth centuries, and in order to generate a spurious race pride among white laborers and thus diffuse labor militancy by stressing color distinctions instead of class distinctions.[14] If nothing else, race relations in the Old South revealed the incredible weakness of the nonslaveholding class and the incredible strength of the ruling planter elite.

So, if the focus is on the antebellum South, the orthodox Marxist's argument that racism and racial stratification were primarily the work of the ruling class is empirically and theoretically sound. A split labor market was created along racial lines, but higher-paid white labor was too powerless to destroy the system of slavery in favor of a racial system that would eliminate or control black competition. The split labor-market theory fails to account for the caste system and the supporting racist ideology imposed by the business elite. But, if the ruling classes were largely responsible for the forms of racial oppression in the antebellum South, it was the workers or nonelite segments of the white population who played a major role in the various forms of racial oppression in the late antebellum North.

Racial Antagonism in the Antebellum North

Recent historical studies lend support to Alexis de Tocqueville's observation during his tour of the United States in the 1830s that "race prejudice seems stronger in those states that have abolished slavery than in those where it still exists, and nowhere is it more intolerant than in those where slavery was never known."[15] Although slavery was abolished in all states above the Mason-Dixon line in the early nineteenth century, this was not the consequence of widespread humanitarian abolitionist sentiment. The downfall of northern slavery was related to more fundamental matters. Unlike in the South, slavery was not central to the more industrial northern economy. The small slave population, which never exceeded seventy thousand in any given period of time, did perform a variety of agricultural and skilled and unskilled mechanical tasks, but slave labor became less essential as cheap European labor became available.[16] Furthermore, only a small percentage of the economically advantaged groups in the North materially or directly benefited from slave labor; therefore, far less pressure was exerted by powerful interest parties for the preservation of slavery. Finally, strong opposition to the use of slave labor in the early nineteenth century came from various groups in the white working population able to develop sufficient power to influence management and political decisions pertaining to the character of the work force. In comparison with their southern counterparts, northern white workers were more concentrated and better organized, and hence more able to protect their economic interests during the antebellum period.[17] The differences in the resources possessed by northern and southern workers were basically related to the different systems of production in the North and in the South. The slave-based plantation economy in the South isolated white workers and facilitated the consolidation of political and economic power among a small elite; in a diversified economy, workers in the North were more centrally involved in the production process, and therefore the power gap between the workers and the capitalist class was not nearly as great.

The abolition of slavery in New England has been attributed largely to the resentment of white labor toward black slaves.[18] Certainly the legislative influence of white labor is well documented. In Pennsylvania, the legislature, reacting to pressure from mechanics, passed a resolution in 1722 decrying the master's custom of hiring out black laborers and mechanics, and in 1726 passed a law prohibiting this practice.[19] The lieutenant governor of New York in 1737 endorsed the complaints of white tradesmen against the use of skilled slave labor and took the matter up with the assembly.[20] In this connection, there has been some speculation that workers formed the backbone of the abolitionist movement to end slavery in the North, but Mandel argues that "the workers had little direct contact with slavery and its consequences, at least until the expansionism of the slaveholder became a national problem. The problem of slavery and the oppressions of the slavocracy did not have for them the immediacy and urgency that they had for the workers in Dixie."[21]

Rather, the most significant opposition to black competition in the Northeastern states occurred after they all had abolished slavery. Violence often flared up where blacks and whites competed for the same jobs, especially during periods of economic depression. Fear of violence and protests by white workers prompted New York City authorities to refuse licenses to black porters and carmen in 1837.[22] Mob protests by unemployed white workers against the hiring of blacks plagued Philadelphia in 1842 and for several years later. These protests inflicted severe economic losses on blacks and "drove so many from the city that the colored population actually showed a decrease at the census of 1850."[23]

The problems faced by northern blacks in the years preceding the Civil War were in no small measure related to the influx of nearly five million European immigrants between 1830 and 1860. The Scandinavian and German immigrants tended to settle on the farmlands in the Midwest and therefore had little direct contact with blacks, but the impoverished Irish immigrants, overwhelmingly concentrated in the slum areas of northern cities, directly competed with blacks for unskilled jobs and cheap housing. The Irish repeatedly voted against proposals to extend political rights to blacks and successfully eliminated blacks from many low-paying occupations. In 1862, for example, "Irish longshoremen informed their employer that all Afro-American longshoreman, dockhands, and other types of workers must be dismissed summarily, otherwise the Irish would tie up the port."[24] After only a few years in the United States, Irish workers gained control of canal and railroad construction and eliminated the black monopoly of the service occupations.[25]

The relative strength of the white laboring class, however, was most clearly evident in the Old Northwest, particularly the states of Ohio, Indiana, and Illinois. The principal settlers of this area were the nonslaveholding whites of the Upper South (Delaware, Kentucky, Maryland, Missouri, North Carolina, Tennessee, and Virginia) who migrated in large measure to escape the political and economic domination of the southern slaveholding elite. Unlike the Lower South (Alabama, Arkansas, Florida, Georgia, Louisiana, Mississippi, South Carolina, and Texas), where nonslaveholding yeomanry tended to be concentrated in the upcountry

and the slaves in the rich black belt or in lowland plantation regions, contact between the nonslaveholders and blacks of the
Upper South was more frequent and competition was therefore
more severe. Artisans and laborers not only had to contend with
the problem of slaves undercutting their economic position, but
they also had to compete with a free black population that by
1860 was six times as large (224,963) as the free black population
of the Lower South (36,955).[26] As artisans, Upper South whites
suffered from competition with skilled slaves, as farmers they
were unable to compete with slaveholders for the most fertile
land, and as laborers they were undercut by both slave labor and
cheaper free black labor. In short, they felt that slavery had
solidified their subordinate position in southern society.[27] For,
as Berwanger has remarked in this connection: "Many settlers
from the South seeking broader economic opportunities migrated
to the Old Northwest because slavery was not permitted there.
Assuming that the land had been reserved for free labor, they
had no intention of legalizing slavery and again establishing a
kind of monopoly of United States land for the slaveholder."[28]
As the careful studies of Berwanger and Voegeli show, not only
did these white laborers successfully resist the extension of slavery into the Old Northwest, but they were also successful in having laws enacted to exclude blacks from entering the area and
in imposing discriminatory barriers to eliminate any possible economic competition from blacks already residing in the area.[29]

It is important to remember, however, that racial antagonism,
although more intense in the Midwest, characterized black and
white interaction throughout the North prior to the Civil War.
Indeed, by 1840, 93 percent of the northern black population resided in states that virtually denied them the right to vote. Negroes' political and judicial rights were severely circumscribed by
statutes and customs, and blacks were relegated to a position of
social inferiority by extralegal codes reinforced by biological
racist norms. The pattern of segregation experienced by Negroes
is summed up vividly by Litwack:

> They were excluded from railway cars, omnibus, stage-
> coaches, and steamboats or assigned to special "Jim Crow"
> sections; they sat, when permitted, in secluded and remote
> corners of theaters and lecture halls; they could not enter

most hotels, restaurants, and resorts, except as servants;
they prayed in "Negro pews" in white churches, and if par-
taking of the sacrament of the Lord's supper, they waited
until the whites had been served the bread and wine.
Moreover, they were often educated in segregated schools,
placed in segregated prisons, nursed in segregated hospitals
and buried in segregated cemeteries.[30]

Although the fear of black competition in the labor market
was most acute among working class groups in the Middle West
and on the East Coast, the greatest reason for white laborers'
antipathy towards blacks was not so much the presence of blacks
in the northern job market but the overriding fear of a black
invasion from the South. Indeed, the violent attacks against
blacks in the famous draft riots in 1860 were prompted by Irish
resentment of being forced to fight a war against the South that
would eventually lead to black emancipation, generate a heavy
influx of blacks into northern areas, and create a serious labor
surplus.[31] Certainly, the political justification of the North's entering the Civil War was not to free the slaves but to restore
the Union after several states had seceded. The Emancipation
Proclamation was issued to free the slaves in the rebellious states
only after northern military and political leaders considered this
historic step necessary to hasten the South's military defeat.

Indeed, certain groups of white workmen were so fearful of
black competition that they openly opposed the emancipation
of slaves. One of the more illuminating statements on this situation has come from Spero and Harris:

> In New York City, the Democratic party . . . [which] pur-
> ported to represent the working class . . . opposed the
> freeing of slaves on the ground that emancipation would
> result in the migration of thousands of blacks to northern
> states, increasing competition for jobs and reducing wages
> even below the level to which an oversupplied labor market
> had already sent them.[32]

There were, however, groups of workers throughout the North,
guided by doctrines of labor solidarity and socialist theory, who
were significantly represented in the antislavery movement.
Unions representing highly skilled German mechanics with so-

cialist backgrounds experienced very little competition from Negro laborers and were especially antislavery. The same was true of the New England Workingman's Association, which expressed the strongest antislavery sentiment among native American workers. The official philosophy of both the German and New England organizations was that workers should be opposed not only to black slavery but also to the "white slavery" of the wage system. The southern slave system was considered as just one phase of the capitalist exploitation of the working class.[33] However, this philosophy represented a minority view among the working classes. Racial or ethnic antagonism in the antebellum North and in the Midwest was never seriously threatened by worker solidarity.

The relationship between social class and different forms of ethnic antagonism is implicit in the foregoing discussion. In the antebellum South, the plantation elite was powerful enough to impose the system of slavery on southern society even though the system was detrimental to the interests of the nonslaveholding white majority. In the North, the laboring classes had the power resources to at least preserve their interests in the face of black competition—and the form of racial subjugation they used reflected their concern, namely, the elimination or neutralization of blacks as economic competitors or potential competitors. As far as black-white relations are concerned, the effective control of black workers by white workers during this period represents a "victory" for higher-paid labor. Evidence from this period lends little support to Marxian explanations that ethnic antagonisms were initiated by the capitalist class. It is true that blacks were used as strikebreakers in isolated incidents, but, since employers had a continuous supply of European immigrant labor, efforts to divide the white and black working class were rarely made. Accordingly, the racial exclusion laws passed in the Old Northwest, the discriminatory acts and legislation against black competition, the support of laws to deny blacks legal and political rights, the stripping of blacks from certain occupations they previously engaged in, the relegation of blacks to the most menial and unskilled positions, and the violence which forced blacks out of certain areas were mainly initiated not by the exploiters of labor but by the white working class.

The efforts of the white working class to deprive Negroes of economic, social, and political resources were certainly made easier by the relatively small Negro population in the North. As we shall see in the following sections, the presence of millions of free blacks following the Civil War presented the southern white working class with a far more difficult challenge, as it attempted to overcome the effects of a century of economic and political subordination in the South.

The Planter Class and Institutionalized Racial Inequality in the Postbellum South

In an argument quite similar to that advanced by Oliver C. Cox in 1948,[34] the Marxist scholars Baran and Sweezy gloss over the mass of historical data with the less than definitive statement that "when Negroes tried to take advantage of their legal freedom to organize along with poor whites in the Populist movement, the planters answered with violence and the Jim Crow system of legalized segregation."[35] As far as the postbellum period is concerned, only if we focus on the period immediately following the Civil War (the period prior to Reconstruction), can we attribute institutionalized racial inequality solely to the planter class. Initial legislation to restrict and control the black population was not generated by white workers, although they were indeed quite concerned about black competition, but by southern planters and their business and political allies.

Immediately following the Civil War, white supremacy, virtually unchallenged during the period of slavery, appeared to be in serious jeopardy. Slaves had been liberated and some were armed. Not only were fears expressed about blacks becoming full citizens and receiving equal political and civil rights, but there was even talk of blacks dividing up the plantation estates. "This was not only competition," states historian C. Vann Woodward, "it looked to many whites like a takeover."[36] More fundamentally, the ruling economic elite was frightened because the southern economy was on the verge of total collapse without slave labor. For the ruling elite, "black freedom" signified not only a threat to white supremacy but also meant the loss of a guaranteed cheap and controlled labor supply for the plantations.

In 1865–66, southern legislatures, still controlled by business and planter groups, were given freedom by Presidents Lincoln and Johnson to devise ways to resolve the problems created by an economy no longer based on slave labor. The legislatures promptly passed a series of discriminatory laws known as the Black Codes. Although the provisions of the codes varied from state to state, one of their primary objectives was to insure an adequate and cheap labor supply for the plantations. Woodward informs us that the "Black Codes of 1865–66 were mainly concerned with forced labor and police laws to get the freedman back to the fields under control."[37] Those blacks without a permanent residence or who were unemployed were classified as vagrants and could be arrested and/or fined, and, if incapable of paying, were bound out to plantations under labor contracts. As a substitute for the social controls of slavery, the codes also restricted black movement, denied blacks political and legal rights, and in some states provided for segregation of certain public facilities.

These escalating efforts to regain control of the black population in the South aroused considerable opposition from many northerners. To some extent, criticism of the Black Codes sprang from lingering abolitionist sentiments generated prior to the Civil War. Northern liberals, in moral indignation, maintained that the Black Codes were a sinister attempt to reestablish slavery. To a greater degree, however, the opposition was political in nature. Benjamin Quarles put the matter squarely:

> As nothing else, the Black Codes played into the hands of the Republicans, who were looking for reasons to postpone the readmission of the southern states. For these states, if readmitted, would elect enough Democrats to insure that party's control of the government. Hence the Republicans were determined to keep the South in political limbo until the ascendancy of their party was assured. To achieve such ascendancy it would be necessary to enfranchise the southern Negro.[38]

In April of 1886, the Republican-controlled Congress nullified the Black Codes by passing a Civil Rights Act which conferred citizenship on ex-slaves and specified that discriminatory acts against them were punishable by fine and/or imprisonment.

Black political and civil rights were further protected by the Fourteenth Amendment passed by Congress in June of 1866. After the Republicans, dominated by the radical wing, had gained a two-thirds majority in both houses in the November election of 1866, Congress passed two supplementary Reconstruction Acts in 1867 that divided the ten southern states into five military districts under northern supervision and that granted blacks the right to vote.[39]

In large measure, white reaction to Reconstruction and the specter of black control of the South was shaped by social class interests. Racial tension increased significantly among lower-class whites who perceived more clearly than ever before the impact of large-scale black competition for low-status jobs. Reconstruction did not destroy the landowning white aristocracy. Both poor whites and blacks were dependent on the planter class for their livelihood as tenants and sharecroppers at the very time when these positions were diminishing in the face of gradual industrialization. The evidence is clear that the planter class of the South effectively prevented any economic or political cooperation or class allegiance between poor blacks and poor whites.[40] As long as poor whites directed their hatred and frustration against the black competitor, the planters were relieved of class hostility directed against them. "Indeed, one motive for the Ku Klux Klan movement of these years was a desire by low class whites to remove the Negro as a competitor, especially in the renting of land."[41] The essential point is that, during the first two decades following the Civil War, poor whites lacked the power resources needed to bring about the kind of institutional changes that would have improved their economic lives, namely, segregationist laws restricting black competition. They were concentrated in positions such as tenant farmers and sharecroppers where their economic situation was as precarious in the early postbellum period as it had been during antebellum slavery. Organized labor remained weak in the face of the overwhelming political and economic resources of the master class.

The reaction of the "people at the top" to the changes in race relations brought about by Reconstruction contrasted sharply with that of lower-class whites. Within a few years after Reconstruction, the ruling economic elite realized that their earlier apprehensions concerning the Negro were unwarranted. Northern Republicans gradually focused their attentions away from their platform of radicalism and protection of black freedom to a promotion of eastern capitalistic expansion in the South.[42] There was greater competition between lower-class whites and blacks and therefore increased racial hostility; but the economic and political hold of the privileged classes over southern life was essentially unchallenged. The plantation elite, aligned with the growing industrial sector, was no longer fearful of a black threat or takeover. Indeed, blacks remained in a dependent economic relationship with this sector. Because of this, and because blacks were anxious about the manifestation of lower-class white reaction to black competition, conservative white rulers virtually controlled the black vote prior to 1890. In this connection, Woodward states:

> It was true that blacks continued to vote in large numbers and to hold minor offices and a few seats in Congress, but this could be turned to account by the conservative white rulers who had trouble with white lower-class rebellion. Black votes could be used to overcome white working-class majorities, and upper-class white protection was needed by blacks under threat of white lower-class aggression. Many reciprocal accommodations between upper-class whites and blacks were possible under the paternalistic order.[43]

The White Labor-Reform Movement and Jim Crow Segregation

Changes in the system of production exerted considerable influence on the developing patterns of class and racial tension in the New South. In the antebellum period, public power was so heavily concentrated among large planters and so clearly derived from property in slaves and land that racial stratification increasingly assumed a paternalistic character that was reflected in the relationships between slaveholders and slaves. This relationship persisted through the early years of the postbellum period. However, as the South experienced gradual industrialization in the late nineteenth century, as new economic institutions generated technological development, as expanded modes of communications and elaborate systems of transportation connected cities with farms, not only was the distribution of power significantly altered in the South but race relations increasingly became associated with class conflicts.[44]

After the Civil War, the planters had to share their power with a rising middle class of merchant-bankers and with owners and operators of factories, mines, and railroads.[45] Nonetheless, the members of all of these groups were conscious of their overlapping economic interests and consequently combined to form a disciplined ruling class. They also were mutually apprehensive of the gradual increase in political activity among the white working class in the 1880s and 1890s. Just as changes in the system of production modified the distribution of power among the ruling elite, so too did it place the workers of the South in greater proximity with one another and thus facilitated their mobilization into collective action groups.

The structural changes in the labor market accompanied severe economic dislocations for many workers of the South. During the last quarter of the nineteenth century, lower-class whites found themselves in increasing contact and competition with millions of freed blacks at the very time that a labor surplus developed in the face of enormous population growth in the South.[46] The problem was especially acute in the Lower South. For the first time, blacks and working-class whites of the Lower South, historically separated in the black belt (lowlands) and the uplands respectively, were forced by economic conditions to confront one another, bump shoulders, and compete on a wide scale for the same jobs. Black youths gradually moved from the lowlands to the new mining and industrial towns of the uplands and found menial, dirty, and low-paying work in tobacco factories, mines, and turpentine camps; meanwhile, sons of white farmers, overwhelmed by debts and falling prices, sifted down from the uplands to the lowlands, where they settled for work in the textile mills or drifted into tenancy. A new breed of southern politician, whose style combined the evangelistic fervor of the southern preacher with the racist rhetoric of the upcountry hillbilly, emerged to articulate the feelings and represent the interests of working-class whites. Their pleas for disfranchisement and legal segregation helped to set in motion a movement that produced decades of Jim Crow segregation.[47] When the Farmers' Alliance, a movement consisting of hundreds of thousands of lower-class white farmers and tenants, first exerted its influence in southern state legislatures, Jim Crow segregation laws sprang up all over the South.[48] For example, in 1887 in Florida, in 1888 in Mississippi, in 1889 in Texas, in 1890 in Louisiana, and in 1891 in Alabama, Arkansas, Kentucky, and Georgia, laws requiring separate accommodations in railway stations and in streetcars were enacted. Perhaps C. Vann Woodward comes closest to summarizing the meaning of these developments when he writes:

> It is one of the paradoxes of Southern history that political democracy for the white man and racial discrimination for the black man were often products of the same dynamics. As the Negroes invaded the new mining and industrial towns of the uplands in greater numbers, and the hill country whites were driven into more frequent and closer association with them, and as the two were brought into rivalry for subsistence wages in the cotton fields, mines and wharves, the lower-class white man's demand for Jim Crow laws became more insistent. . . . The Negro pretty well understood these forces and his grasp of them was one reason for this growing alliance with the most conservative and politically reactionary class of whites against the insurgent white democracy.[49]

Thus, the last decades of the nineteenth century, a period of economic dislocation (caused by industrial capitalism, population pressures, declining farm prices, and exploitative sharecropping) generated a labor reform movement and Jim Crow segregation that grew hand in hand.

Disfranchisement and the Collapse of the Alliance between Blacks and the White Business Elite

The real concern of the business elite in the decade or two following Reconstruction was the threat to its political and economic power by the rise of the agrarian and labor reform movements. It is ironic but not surprising that both the business elite and the black minority were fearful of the rise in white lower-class power. The unholy alliance between blacks and the white ruling classes prior to 1890 actually prevented the racial code from becoming more severe.

As long as the alliance between blacks and the conservative economic elite existed, the latter frequently denounced Jim Crow laws in aristocratic, paternalistic tones as "unnecessary and un-called for" and "a needless affront to our respectable and well behaved colored people."[50] According to Woodward, "when the first state Jim Crow law for trains was passed in 1887, a conserva-tive paper rather shamefacedly admitted it was done 'to please the crackers.' "[51]

However, at the very time that Jim Crow legislation was mush-rooming throughout the South, some workers in the Populist movement recognized that as long as conservative whites were aligned with blacks, the possibility of a united working-class labor movement to overcome economic exploitation would in-deed be difficult. The Populists sought strenuously to create an alliance with poor blacks. Under the leadership of Tom Watson, a substantial Populist appeal to the black man was generated in Georgia. Some successes also occurred in Texas and Arkansas.[52] This was enough to alarm the conservative Democrats represent-ing the southern business interests, and they too increased their drive to attract the support of black voters, using methods that included the stuffing of ballot boxes with fraudulent votes in the black-belt regions. Both the Populists and the Democrats sought to manipulate the black vote, and both finally realized that since neither was assured of controlling the black vote, "it was much better to have clear-cut constitutional disfranchisement of the Negro and to leave the white group to fight elections out among themselves."[53]

The conservative Democrats of the lowland South, who, when they felt secure about the black vote, had placed the blame for the rise of legal segregation on lower-class whites, joined in the movement for disfranchisement as soon as they became appre-hensive about the black vote.[54] Meanwhile, white Republicans of the South were divided over the issue of disfranchisement. "The lily-white faction, which gained ground during the nineties, more or less openly welcomed the movement in the belief that the removal of the Negro would make the party respectable in the South and permit white men to divide."[55] Between 1890 and 1910, blacks were systematically disfranchised by various pro-cedures ranging from the revising of state constitutions to re-

quiring poll taxes, literacy tests, and property qualifications, to
the creation of the all-white Democratic primary (which was far
more important than the general election because the South was
dominated by a one-party system).[56] Accompanying disfranchisement were increased Jim Crow segregation laws in both public
and private institutions and facilities and also the virtual collapse
of public education and the systematic exclusion by white laborers of blacks from jobs in the skilled occupational ranks they had
held since slavery (such as barbering, masonry, bricklaying, car-
pentry, and the better agricultural jobs).[57] Moreover, the system
of Jim Crow segregation was reinforced by extralegal means of
intimidation. Whereas, blacks were seldom lynched under the
old paternalistic order (e.g., as I indicated in the previous chapter, it is estimated that of the 300 lynching victims between 1840
and 1860 less than 10 percent were black)[58] "in the last sixteen
years of the nineteenth century there had been more than 2,500
lynchings, the great majority of which were Negroes, with Mississippi, Alabama, Georgia, and Louisiana leading the nation."[59]

White Economic Class Interests and Black Subordination

Restrictive arguments that the Jim Crow system was the work of
the capitalist class, or was due solely to the victory of higher-
paid white labor, obscure the dynamics of the complex patterns
of racial inequality in the postbellum South. I have attempted to
show, and historical analysis demonstrates, that: (1) the initial
form of racial stratification in the postbellum period, formalized
and sanctioned by the Black Codes, was based solely on the
efforts of the plantation elite to insure an adequate and cheap
labor supply for the plantations in the aftermath of slave emancipation. Racial inequality therefore reflected the class interests of
the aristocracy and entailed the exploitation of labor. (2) The
emergence of initial Jim Crow segregation laws directly parallels
the rise of lower-class whites to political power in the labor reform movement. Racial inequality therefore reflected the class
interests of white workers and was designed to eliminate black
encroachment in a context of competitive race relations. (3) The
political alliance and paternalistic bond between blacks and the
business classes deteriorated in the face of the Populist challenge;

this deterioration causing the struggle over the black vote to result in a more united white movement to deprive the Negroes of their political rights. (4) The racial caste system which encompassed all aspects of black life was solidified both by the ruling class's support of disfranchisement and by the working class's drive (with tacit approval of the ruling class) toward racial exclusiveness in occupation, education, and political power.

Conclusion

In this chapter I have attempted to show how the different contexts of racial antagonism in the preindustrial and early industrial periods restrict the uniform application of the economic class theories discussed previously. Because they do not focus on the influence of different systems of production on the intergroup arena, the economic class theories are unable to account for the fundamental relationship between changes in the power resources possessed by antagonistic classes and changes in the nature of racial interaction. Thus, whereas the orthodox Marxist explanation is restricted to the racial caste system in the antebellum South and the development of the Black Codes in the immediate post–Civil war period, the split labor-market theory can only be used to explain racial stratification in the late antebellum North and the origins of Jim Crow segregation in the postbellum South. Again, the meaningful application of the economic class arguments in any given historical period depends heavily on the knowledge of the constraints imposed by the particular systems of production during that period, constraints that help to shape the structural relations between racial and class groups and which thereby produce different patterns of intergroup interaction.[60]

As long as the reservoir of free white workers was not central to the reproduction of labor supply in the southern plantation economy, slavery as a mode of production facilitated the consolidation and concentration of economic power in the hands of the slaveholders. The control of the economic system was effectively transferred to the control of the political and legal systems as the slaveholders used their political power to protect their class interests in slavery. The polity therefore reinforced and regulated the system of racial caste oppression and made it difficult for either blacks or lower-class whites to mount any serious challenge to the institution of slavery. In short, the economy provided the basis for the development of the racial caste system, and the polity reinforced and perpetuated that system. Moreover, the economy enabled the slaveholders to develop a regional center of power and the polity legitimated that power.

In the antebellum North, where a more industrial system of production enabled white workers to become more concentrated and better organized, laws of racial oppression, especially in the nineteenth century, increasingly reflected the interests of the white working class. The demise of northern slavery was quickly followed by laws to eliminate black competition, particularly economic competition. However, as the economy of the South gradually drifted toward industrial capitalism in the last quarter of the nineteenth century, the white working classes there were finally able to exert some influence on the form and content of racial stratification. White working-class efforts to eliminate black competition generated an elaborate system of Jim Crow segregation that was reinforced by an ideology of biological racism. The white working class was aided not only by its numerical size but also by its increasing accumulation of political resources that accompanied changes in its relations to the means of production; in other words, it was aided by its gradual transformation of increasing labor power into increasing political power.

4 INDUSTRIAL EXPANSION AND DISPERSED RACIAL CONFLICT

During the late nineteenth century, while class conflicts and racial tensions in the South were producing a rigid system of racial segregation, in the North, ironically, an unprecedented period of racial amity and integration was prevailing, especially between 1870 and 1890.[1] The improved racial situation was evidenced by the proliferation of civil rights laws passed by state legislatures. Between 1873 and 1885 fourteen states had passed one or more laws barring discrimination in public places. In New York state, for instance, civil rights laws gave blacks the right to vote without interference, eat in restaurants, use transportation facilities, attend theaters, and be buried in public cemeteries. Furthermore, New York state declared interracial marriages legal and outlawed the practice of discriminatory insurance rates. Negroes began serving as jurymen in Manhattan in the 1880s; the traditions of de jure separate education in New York City was ended in 1884 as the last three Negro public schools became ward schools; the first permanent appointment of a black teacher to a predominantly white school in New York City was made in 1895; finally, a statewide education act passed in 1900 gave the coup de grace to separate black education.[2] "Negro and white people were aware of the changes in racial status typified by these acts," states Osofsky. "Cases of discrimination in public places continued to occur, but it was generally recognized that significant progress was made in the area of race relations subject to law since the end of the Civil War."[3]

It was not uncommon to find racially mixed residential areas in northern cities between 1870 and 1890. For example, in Chicago, prior to 1900, one would rarely find a solidly black block, and a significant number of Negroes lived in white neighborhoods. Although a color line continued to restrict black employment opportunities, "exceptional black people did succeed in business and the professions—frequently hailed by whites and blacks alike as indications of the 'progress of the race.' "[4]

It is probably true that the lingering spirit of racial reform which had developed during the Civil War and Reconstruction periods influenced the way northern blacks were perceived and treated.[5] But, more fundamental and important factors shaped the quality of race relations in the 1870s, 1880s, and 1890s. Unlike in the pre–Civil War period, when black workers were in direct competition with lower-status European immigrants for menial positions, there was little racial competition during the late nineteenth century because the German and Irish immigrants had significantly improved their economic status in the trades and municipal employment. They therefore had little occupational contact with blacks, who were concentrated on the lower rungs of the occupational ladder. Since blacks were not perceived as a major economic threat by white workers, and since they constituted a rather small proportion of the total population, they tended to be relatively invisible to the white masses. The foreign-born white population constituted 39.7 percent of the total population in New York City in 1880, but blacks comprised only 1.6 percent (19,663). In Chicago, the figures were 40.7 percent foreign-born and only 1.3 percent (6,480) black. In Philadelphia, 24.1 percent were foreign-born and 3.7 percent (31,699) were black. And, in Boston, 31.6 percent of the population were foreign-born but only 1.6 percent (5,873) were black.

This remarkable period of fluid race relations proved to be short-lived. During the 1890s, there were indications that racial tolerance was giving way to intolerance and that racial amity was losing ground to racial tension. By 1900, it had become apparent to any sensitive observer that the issue was not whether Negroes would continue to experience improvements in basic civil and human rights, but whether they would be able to retain the few rights and privileges they had attained during the three previous decades. Residential segregation increased sharply as blacks were driven out of white communities "by neighborhood improvement associations, economic boycotts, frequent acts of violence, and later, restrictive covenants."[6] Civil rights laws were substantially ineffectual, due to lack of enforcement and to refusal of white juries to uphold them. And following 1900, the probability of a white constituency electing a black man to public office during the period of industrial race relations declined to nearly zero. "In Chicago, for instance, blacks had been elected to the state legislature and to the county board of commissioners by predominantly white constituencies in the 1880s and the early 1890s. In 1906, however, when a black attorney ran for municipal court, he aroused vigorous white opposition and was the only Republican candidate to lose in what was otherwise a Republican sweep."[7]

After 1900, in New York City, there was a sharp increase in the number of legal suits brought by blacks against white discrimination in hotels, restaurants, and theaters. Indeed, the poisonous racial atmosphere permeated all major institutions. White churches, which had allowed small numbers of blacks to participate in their services in the 1870s and 1880s, attempted to ease out black members altogether.[8] Racial conflict between blacks and working-class whites also intensified. Many of the more serious incidents were related to labor disputes, when employers used black strikebreakers to undermine the predominantly white labor-union movement. It really did not matter that blacks represented only a small percentage of the strikebreakers, for as Spero and Harris noted in this connection:

> The Negro always stands out in the crowd. His color makes this inevitable. The presence of a dozen black men in a force of strikebreakers appears to the strikers like a hundred. During the celebrated teamsters' strike of 1905, in Chicago, it was estimated that 5,800 strike breakers were used throughout the summer to fill the places of 5,000 strikers. Of these 5,800 strike breakers, 5,000 were white. Yet the Negro was signaled out for special violence and abuse. The papers printed exaggerated accounts of imported Negroes taking the places of white men, and aroused the public to a fever pitch of racial feelings. As a matter of fact, the white strike breakers brought into Chicago from outside during this dispute outnumbered the Negro by more than seven to one.[9]

The deterioration of race relations in the North, together with the crystallization of Jim Crow segregation in the South at the turn of the century derived from fundamental economic, social, and demographic changes in the American society. This period was characterized by rapid urbanization and urban dislocation, industrial strife, and internal migration and disrupted patterns of living. The radically increased migration of rural southern blacks to the industrial centers of the North, stimulated by basic changes in the system of production, greatly exacerbated economic and social anxieties and profoundly affected the quality of urban race relations.

Black Migration and Changes in the System of Production

Over 90 percent of the Negroes in the United States lived below the Mason-Dixon line prior to 1900. Concentrated mainly in rural areas, they experienced living conditions considerably inferior to those of northern blacks. Although the North also presented significant problems for blacks, in the final analysis the Negro there could receive greater economic opportunities, experience more freedom as a human being, and enjoy greater security as a citizen, especially between 1870 and 1890. In the South, on the other hand, a foundation for a rigid pattern of Jim Crow segregation and disfranchisement had been laid. In the wake of the white lower classes' efforts to assert greater control over their economic lives, lynchings and general white intimidation sharply increased in the 1870s and 1880s. Furthermore, an enormous southern population growth created a huge labor surplus. In the face of this, Negroes were denied jobs in the new cotton industries of the Southwest and whites began to infringe on traditionally "Negro jobs." "Except for a small proportion of Negro professionals and businessmen who served their own people," writes Gunnar Myrdal, "few Negroes in the South had opportunity to improve their economic position. At least in a subjective sense— which is the important thing in discussing human motivation— the difference in desirability between South and North widened as Southern Negroes became more educated and came to know the outside world better."[10] Because of the surplus of immigrant labor, prior to World War I Negroes in the North were denied industrial employment, except as strikebreakers; however, they could easily find service jobs. Indeed, in many parts of the North, it was fashionable to hire Negro domestic help instead of European immigrants.[11]

Despite the superior advantages of life in the North, black migration from the South increased only gradually throughout the late nineteenth century and did not begin to reach significant numbers until the World War I period (table 2). Gunnar Myrdal is probably correct when he asserts that "there was before 1915 an existing and widening difference in living conditions between South and North which did not express itself in a mass migration simply because the latter did not get a start and become a pattern."[12]

TABLE 2. Net Migration to and from the South by Color and Decade, 1870–1960 (in 1,000's)

	Total South			Southeast (11 States)		
Decade	Total	White	Non-white	Total	White	Non-white
1870–1880	+11	+82	−71	−304	−205	−99
1880–1890	−411	−328	−83	−515	−405	−110
1890–1900	−143	+52	−195	−849	−537	−312
1900–1910	−274	−77	−197	−872	−605	−267
1910–1920	−1,088	−566	−522	−1,219	−642	−577
1920–1930	−1,576	−704	−872	−1,704	−778	−926
1930–1940	−756	−349	−407	−651	−188	−463
1940–1950	−2,135	−538	−1,599	−1,880	−365	−1,515
1950–1960	−1,403	+53	−1,456	−1,078	+381	−1,459
Totals	−7,777	−2,375	−5,402	−9,072	−3,344	−5,728

Source: Adapted from C. Horace Hamilton, "The Negro Leaves the South," *Demography* 1, no. 1 (1964): 279.

Several factors created what Myrdal has called a "shock effect" that intensified the migration of blacks from the South in the second decade of the twentieth century. There was a "push" from the South and a "pull" from the North; and, in each instance, the issues were reduced to essentially economic considerations. The push factor was a rise in the Negro's economic insecurity produced by the declining demand for farm labor due to increasing mechanization in agriculture and to more comprehensive methods of agriculture. Between 1914 and 1917, cotton production was severely hampered by boll-weevil infestation and by a series of storms and floods that wiped out many crops. These disasters created both severe hardships for Negro farmers and wage cuts and unemployment for blacks in urban factories related to the cotton industry. Furthermore, white workers, suffering from the depressed economic system, "infiltrated" into jobs that blacks had monopolized for decades.

If there was a push of economic deprivation from the South, there was also a pull of opportunity from the North. Throughout the latter half of the nineteenth century, northern industrialists had tended to ignore black workers, primarily because the immigration of European ethnics provided them with an adequate and continuous cheap labor supply. It was therefore much easier, and not unprofitable, for industrialists to adhere to explicit racial norms of unequal treatment for blacks and to satisfy white workers' demands that Negroes be excluded from industry. However, as I indicated in Chapter 1, if conformity to traditional racial norms results in significant economic losses, industrialists are much more likely to break with precedent. Indeed, when World War I immigration restrictions reduced the annual average migration from Europe (particularly the unskilled immigrants from southern and eastern Europe) from over a million (1910 to 1914) to roughly one hundred thousand (1915 to 1920), and when the demands of the war economy increased the gross national product and expanded the need for manufacturing employment, employers literally begged Negroes to work in the steel mills, the railroads, the automobile factories, and the cotton industries. Young reports that there was not a single industry "in which some shortage of labor did not develop in the semiskilled ranks in one locality or another."[13] Labor recruiters from northern firms circulated throughout the South offering black laborers free transportation and high wages if they agreed to work in industrial plants.

The Chicago Commission on Race Relations reported that, during an eighteen-month period, more than fifty thousand Negroes arrived in Chicago.[14] From 1910 to 1920, the black population of Chicago increased by 148.2 percent (65,355 to 109,458), of Pittsburgh by 117.1 percent (9,190 to 20,355), of New York by 66.3 percent (60,758 to 152,467), of Philadelphia by 58.9 percent (25,894 to 69,854), and of St. Louis by 58.9 percent (25,894 to 69,854). Similar gains were shown in almost all the second-line northern industrial cities, such as Indianapolis, Kansas City, and Columbus.[15] "When factors of inertia were once overcome and the northward mass migration was started," states Myrdal, "the movement quickly took on momentum. A new pattern of behavior was set; a new hope in the possibilities in the North was created. Lines of communication between North and South were established."[16]

In the decade of the 1920s, the net black migration from the South to the North and West was 872,000. This represented an increase of over 250,000 from the previous decade (see table 2). Many of the factors associated with Negro migration prior to and during World War I continued to facilitate the black trek to the cities. After a brief postwar depression, the economy greatly expanded and northern industries were booming. Immigration laws kept the flow of eastern and southern European immigrants to a mere trickle, thereby forcing industrialists to tap the industrial reserve of Negroes for unskilled labor. And, in the early 1920s, the cotton industry in the South Atlantic and South Central states was on the wane.

Although black migration from the South was considerably reduced in the 1930s, still over four hundred thousand Negroes left the region. Despite the fact that the depression of the 1930s virtually eliminated job opportunities and that Negroes in the North were being laid off by the thousands, the "push" factors from the South were probably operating at an even greater force than previously. The Depression, which increased competition from other cotton-producing countries, and the growing use of cotton substitutes drastically reduced the demand for cotton, both at home and abroad. Two other cash crops—tobacco and sugar—also suffered because of a sharp drop in national and international consumption. But the setback in the cotton industry had the most severe impact upon the Negro, because, as Myrdal points out, "cotton is one of the most labor consuming crops in the South."[17] The problems of Negro farmers and farm workers were compounded when the Agricultural Adjustment Program was introduced in 1933 to raise and stabilize farm income by limiting cash-crop acreages, removing price-depressing surpluses from regular markets, paying direct subsidies to farmers who mechanized their farming, and encouraging conservation practices. This drive toward modernization and conservation effectively phased out many Negro sharecroppers and tenant farmers, and thousands sought economic relief in the cities even though the prospects for jobs were not encouraging.[18]

The technological revolution in southern agriculture rapidly expanded through the 1940s and early 1950s. Some areas experienced a 100 percent per annum growth in new technology. "Mechanization was introduced in stages," observes Richard H. Day, "first affecting land preparation and cultivation as tractor power displaced mules, then handweeding as flame throwers and herbicides were applied, and finally harvesting as mechanical cotton pickers replaced the sharecropper and his family."[19] A good deal of the labor released was absorbed by the expanding industrial centers of the North from the beginning of World War II, through the post-war boom, to the end of the Korean War. Indeed, in response to the "pull" of new and widening employment opportunities in manufacturing cities of the North and the expanding defense industries on the West Coast, the net migration of blacks from the South during the 1940s swelled to nearly 1,600,000.

The net migration decreased, however, to slightly less than 1,500,000 during the 1950s. This drop in the migration rate could not be attributed to any reduction in the "push" pressures from the South. On the contrary, the increasing mechanization was forcing Negroes out of agricultural work at an unprecedented rate. For example, in the three years from 1949 to 1952, unskilled agricultural labor declined by 72 percent in twenty Mississippi delta counties, and by 1957 it had dropped to 10 percent of the level recorded in 1949.[20] The problem continued into the 1960s, and its effects on black workers was vividly described by Michael J. Piore in late 1967:

> The plight of Negroes in the Delta today is the result of changes in the economic system. Suddenly in the space of two years, the Negro part of the economy has been eliminated. In the spring of 1960, seasonal employment in the Mississippi Delta totaled 30,510; in the spring of 1965, it was 32,328. Last year, spring seasonal employment was cut almost in half, from 32,328 to 16,571. This spring it fell by over half again to 7,225. Seasonal employment in the fall exhibits a comparable trend. . . . Incomes of Negroes in the Delta have been among the lowest in the nation, but today, numbers of families have no income at all. What was

once malnutrition and accumulated disease has become
virtual starvation. Even in the summer months, many families
were begging from door to door.[21]

Thus the continuous decline in opportunities for Negroes in
agriculture since 1910 has had the effect of "pushing" blacks
from rural southern areas to urban areas in enormous numbers.
Although some blacks sought economic relief in southern cities,
most migrated to the burgeoning industrial centers of the North
where job opportunities and public services were greater.
Throughout the twentieth century, industrialization in the South
lagged considerably behind the development of northern industry. Before 1950, racial discrimination effectively prevented significant black employment in the manufacturing sector of the
urban South. In view of the available and more than adequate
supply of white workers, many of whom were also driven from
the farms by mechanization, employers saw little need to challenge the racial barriers institutionalized by Jim Crow segregation.

The heavy migration of rural southern blacks to the urban centers of the North and the West, and, to a lesser but increasingly
significant extent, to the cities of the South, transformed black
Americans from an overwhelmingly rural population in 1890 (80
percent rural and 20 percent urban) to an essentially urban population in 1950 (62 percent urban and 38 percent rural). And, by
1970, the proportion of blacks residing in urban areas had swelled
to 81 percent (see table 3).

I shall delay a discussion of the effects of this population
change on race relations in the modern industrial period and, in
the remaining sections of this chapter, focus specifically on the
patterns of racial antagonism associated with black population
shifts in the latter phase of the industrial period of race relations
(that is, in the first two quarters of the twentieth century).

Growth of the Black Urban Population and Conflict in
the Industrial Order

Prior to the World War I period, very few blacks were employed
in the nation's industrial plants. In the South, where before the
Civil War blacks had successfully competed with whites in nearly

every branch of industry, black labor had become restricted largely to agricultural work and to personal services. Organized white-worker resistance, reinforced by norms of racial exclusion that crystallized with the emergence of Jim Crow segregation, effectively prevented the free employment of black labor in industry. Moreover, since southern industry developed slowly throughout the late nineteenth and early twentieth centuries, the

TABLE 3. Proportion of Blacks Living in Urban and Rural Areas, 1890–1970

Decade	Total United States		South		North and West	
	Urban	Rural	Urban	Rural	Urban	Rural
1890	20%	80%	15%	85%	62%	38%
1900	23	77	17	83	70	30
1910	27	73	21	79	77	23
1920	34	66	25	75	84	16
1930	44	56	32	68	88	12
1940	49	51	37	64	89	11
1950	62	38	48	52	93	7
1960	73	27	58	42	95	5
1970	81	19	67	33	97	3

Source: U.S. Bureau of the Census, *Census of the Population, 1970,* Race of the Population for Regions, Divisions, and States, 1970, Table 60 (Washington, D.C.: Government Printing Office).

demand for labor could be readily satisfied by the surplus of white workers. In the North, as long as there was access to cheap immigrant labor, the industrialists made little effort to attract black workers, except in special situations such as strikes or acute labor shortages. In fact, the first significant efforts to tap the reserve of rural workers occurred only when both native and immigrant workers organized and struck.

It was no coincidence that management's increasing tendency to use blacks as strikebreakers occurred during the period when Negroes began to migrate from rural to urban areas in significant numbers. The difficulty of securing an adequate living in the rural South made many blacks receptive to overtures from white industrialists. They therefore did not hesitate to cross the picket line. Thus, for example, the entry of blacks into northern steel mills from 1875 to 1914 was chiefly in the capacity of strikebreakers.[22] As indicated in Table 4, blacks were used to break strikes in various industries throughout the first three decades of the twentieth century.

TABLE 4. Strikes in Which Blacks Were Used as Strikebreakers, 1916–1934

Industry	Year	Locality
Aluminum	1917	East St. Louis
Brick-making	1923	Newark
Building	1919	New York
Coal mining	1922	Pennsylvania
	1925	Northern West Virginia
	1927	Western Pennsylvania
	1928	Ohio
	1934	Birmingham
Corn refining	1919	Chicago
Fig and date packing	1926	Chicago
Garment industry	1917	Chicago
	1920	Chicago
Hotel industry	1918	Chicago
Longshore work	1916	Baltimore
	1923	New Orleans
	1929	Boston
Meat-packing	1916	East St. Louis
	1919	Chicago
	1921	Chicago
	1921	Widespread
Metal trades	1921	Detroit
Railroads	1916	Chicago
	1922	Unspecified
Restaurants	1920	Chicago
Steel	1919	Widespread

Source: Adapted from Edna Bonacich, "Advanced Capitalism and Black-White Relations in the United States; A Split Labor Market Interpretation," *American Sociological Review* 41 (February 1976): 41.

The significance of black strikebreaking is not that it provided an early opportunity for Negroes to enter northern industries (because, as I have shown, the really important breakthrough for blacks occurred when they were hired on a permanent and regular basis during the labor shortage periods of the World War I era), but that it created incidents that dramatically revealed and directly contributed to a racially charged atmosphere. Indeed, whether blacks were used as strikebreakers or whether they were simply hired on a regular basis, their movement into industry sharply exacerbated not only the economic and social anxieties of the white working class but also their racial antagonism. "Nearly every overt racial clash in the North in the early twentieth century involved conflict between blacks and working class whites," states Allen Spear. "In many instances labor disputes led directly to attacks on black workers by white strikers and their sympathizers."[23] It cannot be overemphasized that racial conflicts between workers derived from a more general problem of economic dislocation. Conflict between management and workers over labor disputes was widespread at this time. Thus the growing presence of black workers in urban industries, coupled with the tendency of management to use blacks as strikebreakers to undercut effective union activity, created a situation where the class conflict between white labor and management produced racial conflict between white workers and blacks. This point requires some amplification.

Most of the black workers who migrated to the northern industrial centers went directly into low-paying, unskilled or semi-skilled work in the automobile plants, steel mills, packinghouses, and foundries. Some entered construction jobs requiring little or no skill; and still others, including many women, were employed in the unskilled branches of needle trades, food industries, and commercial laundries.[24] What was distinctive about these jobs, however, is that both native and Americanized foreign-born white workers tended to reject them in favor of more desirable employment. As Spero and Harris observe, "This largely accounts for the almost spectacular increase in the proportion of Negroes in the iron and steel foundries where the work is dirty, hot and unpleasant. The foundries and metal works in the Chicago district and in the Middle West generally began to employ Negro labor between 1916 and 1921 when they could no longer get an adequate supply of foreign workers, although some had been experimenting with Negro labor before that time."[25] The relegation of blacks to the least desirable jobs in industry helped to perpetuate the traditional separation of jobs into racial categories. In the early twentieth century, Negroes had little or no chance to break the white monopoly on such blue-collar jobs as locomotive engineer, railroad conductor, motorman, or subway guard. Also, union restrictions effectively barred them from many of the skilled crafts.

The fact that blacks were concentrated in the least desirable industrial jobs did not weaken white worker opposition to their employment. If nothing else, blacks constituted a potential threat to the more desirable jobs and provided management with leverage to maintain depressed wages. Only in those plants in which labor organizations had little or no influence on management's hiring practices were blacks able to penetrate racial barriers. These tended to be industries that relied heavily on unskilled and semiskilled labor, labor which could be easily performed by unskilled black workers. It was not without some justification, then, that Negro leaders frequently sided with management in labor disputes and counseled blacks to become strikebreakers.[26]

The use of blacks as strikebreakers was only one of the ways in which the employers' use of black labor threatened the interests of white labor. In some situations, management negated the demands of white workers by replacing them permanently with black labor. For example, in 1916, following a brief strike, the Aluminum Ore Company of East St. Louis discharged a large number of white workers and replaced them with black labor. From November 1916 to February 1917, the number of black workers in the plant increased from roughly a dozen to 470.[27] Management efforts to thwart the demands of white labor also accounted for increases in black labor in the meat-packing and bituminous coal industries in the early twentieth century.[28] Moreover, as Bonacich points out, "displacement was sometimes accompanied by efforts to gain the loyalty of the black work force, thereby forestalling the development of unions among them and maintaining the 'cheap labor status.' "[29] In this connection, many of the largest industrial agencies contributed substantially to the local chapters of the National Urban League because of its open hostility to white labor unions and willingness to supply industry with black strikebreakers. "Industries regarded the local League as a useful agency for procuring labor and as a conservative stabilizing force in the colored community."[30]

The heavy migration of blacks to urban centers and their encroachment on northern industries presented problems for white workers, and these difficulties were not confined to the labor market. The expanding black urban population created housing shortages in many urban communities as blacks spilled over ghetto boundaries into ethnic working-class communities. The racial tensions that ensued certainly were not relieved when landlords capitalized on the situation by quickly raising rents. Furthermore, as blacks and whites experienced more frequent contacts and encounters outside their homes, neighborhoods, and workplaces, racial antagonism based on competition for scarce social facilities, such as bathing beaches, parks, and playgrounds, was not uncommon.[31]

Two decades of growing racial hostility culminated in the outbreak of interracial riots in East St. Louis in 1917 and in Chicago and over twenty other cities in 1919, as black and white citizens fought openly in racial warfare. In the East St. Louis riot, forty-eight people (nine whites and thirty-nine blacks) lost their lives, hundreds were injured, and more than three hundred buildings were destroyed. In the Chicago riot of 1919, the death toll was thirty-eight (fifteen whites and twenty-three blacks), over five hundred injured, and roughly a thousand homeless or destitute.[32] As the nation experienced economic recovery during the 1920s, the extreme tensions of the World War I period subsided. Yet there were occasional interracial flareups after that period, the most serious of which was the Detroit riot of 1943 (twenty-three blacks and fifteen whites killed).[33] All of these outbursts were products of social anxieties created by industrial strife, urban dislocation, and population shifts. Describing the more serious outbreaks that occurred in East St. Louis in 1917, in Chicago in 1919, and in Detroit in 1943, Rudwick states:

> During the years immediately preceding its race riot each city experienced large increases in Negro population primarily because of the influx from the South. Between 1910 and 1917 the East St. Louis community grew from nearly 6,000 to perhaps as many as 13,000. In Chicago there were nearly 110,000 Negroes in 1920 compared to 44,000 a decade earlier. Detroit in 1940 had about 160,000 Negro residents, but three years later there were an estimated 220,000 Negroes. . . . In all three cities, unskilled whites manifested tension after they considered their jobs threat-

ened by Negroes. There was also concern because migrants had overburdened the housing and transportation facilities. Everywhere, efforts of Negroes to improve their status were defined as arrogant assaults, and whites insisted on retaining competitive advantages enjoyed before the Negro migration. Economic conflict was inevitable because the industrial corporations had employed Negroes not only to supplement white labor but also to crush strikes and destroy unions.[34]

In the final analysis, the rioting served to underscore the effect of economic changes on the interracial arena, as all of the major interracial riots had either a direct or indirect connection with industrial strife.[35] However, during and immediately following the New Deal era there were also a force at work that ultimately contributed to a nationwide reduction of racial strife in the industrial sector after World War II, namely, the gradual absorption of blacks into labor unions, particularly the industry-wide unions such as the Congress of Industrial Organizations (CIO).

Management-Labor Conflicts and the Absorption of Negroes into Industry-Wide Unions

The growth of the labor movement during the early twentieth century generated a vigorous antiunion campaign by management which included court injunctions and other legal maneuvers, antiunion publicity, infiltration of the union movement with labor spies, importation of both black and white strikebreakers, blacklisting and arbitrary dismissal of union members, and coercive tactics to break strikes and keep out organizers. The effects of these campaigns were very nearly catastrophic for the nation's labor unions, as union membership declined sharply during the 1920s.[36] "With few exceptions, only the strong craft unions in the construction, printing and railroad industries were able to survive these setbacks" observed Ray Marshall. "Moreover, with few exceptions . . . the kinds of unions that survived these adverse conditions were likely to be the stronger organizations which practiced hostile discrimination against the Negro."[37]

The economic hardships of the Great Depression sharply increased workers' motivation to unionize, and the prounion New

Deal policies of the Franklin D. Roosevelt administration provided the legal protection needed to organize. Shortly before Roosevelt took office, Congress passed the Norris-LaGuardia Act, which significantly limited the use of court injunctions against striking, boycotting, and picketing. The act also included a clause outlawing "yellow dog" contracts (a binding contract between employer and worker whereby the latter would agree, as a condition of employment, not to join or remain in a union). In the New Deal period, the National Industrial Recovery Act (NIRA) of 1933 provided a tremendous psychological boost to unionizing activity. Section 7a of the NIRA stipulated that workers have "the right to organize and bargain collectively through representatives of their own choosing, and shall be free from the interference, restraint, or coercion of employers of labor." Although declared unconstitutional in 1936, the NIRA had by then accelerated unionization of labor organizations. Moreover, section 7a of the NIRA was essentially embodied in the Wagner Act of 1935, which rendered illegal certain unfair labor practices that were undermining unions, granted workers the right to vote for their selected bargaining representatives, and established and empowered a National Labor Relations Board to enforce the act.[38]

Protective legislation thus provided a favorable climate for union organization, facilitating, for example, the formation of the CIO by dissident labor leaders who felt that the American Federation of Labor (AFL) was not sufficiently responsive to the opportunities for union growth. The split between the CIO and AFL proved to be especially timely for black workers because the new protective legislation supporting collective bargaining (that is, the selection of labor representatives on the basis of workers' votes) prompted both organizations to compete openly for the black vote. As Marshall has commented, the change in racial practices "was inevitable in view of the large number of Negroes employed in the steel, auto, mining, packinghouse, rubber and other mass-producing industries which were primary targets of CIO organizing activities."[39] Indeed, from the very beginning, CIO officials embraced an equalitarian racial policy that actually "caused the AFL and its affiliates to relax some of their racial restrictions."[40] It was true that some of the CIO unions practiced racial discrimination by either barring blacks altogether, permitting segregated locals, or tolerating restriction of blacks to inferior jobs. Nonetheless, the racial policies of industry-wide unions contrasted sharply with the craft unions which, because they were able to exercise greater control over the racial make-up of their membership (workers were organized on the basis of individual crafts), remained racially exclusive throughout and following the New Deal era.[41] On the whole, however, the New Deal period marked the beginning of a substantial structural change in the relationship between black and white workers. The growing entry of blacks into the CIO and other mass production industries decreased black hostility towards unions, virtually eliminated management's practice of hiring nonunion blacks as strikebreakers, and significantly reduced the tensions and hostilities between white and black workers. August Meier and Elliot Rudwick convey the significance of these developments in their assessment of the impact of the CIO's racial policy: "It made interracial trade unionism truly respectable. It gave black and white workers a sense of common interests, a solidarity that transcended racial lines."[42] But a discussion of the changes in black-white relations in the economic sector provides only a partial view of the dynamics of race relations during the industrial period. Despite the fact that blacks gradually increased their participation in labor unions and in industries, they could not significantly penetrate racial barriers imposed by the urban political machines.

The Ghetto and the Urban Political System

Comparisons drawn between blacks and European immigrant groups during the first half of the twentieth century can hardly overlook the differences in their respective positions in and relations with the urban political machines.[43] Since substantial black migration did not occur before World War I, by 1920 blacks were already several decades behind European immigrant ethnics in developing institutional capabilities for urban life. The German and Irish began their migration to the United States in significant numbers in the 1840s; the Italians and the Jews descended on the cities from 1880 through the first two decades of the twentieth century; blacks, on the other hand, did not migrate to urban areas in large numbers until after World War I, with the largest migration occurring between 1940 and 1960.

The belated entry of blacks from the South to the cities of the North and West left these migrants without the sociopolitical influence that the cities had provided other groups during much of the early twentieth century. Although this accounts in part for the fact that black Americans have not developed the degree of political influence characteristic of the major ethnic groups, it does not sufficiently explain the slower and later rate of growth in political power among urbanized blacks in contrast to the white ethnics.

Far more important was the fact that no other immigrant group—neither the Irish, the Italians, the Jews, nor the Polish— faced the degree of systematic exclusion from the urban political system as did the blacks. It is true that unlike in the South, blacks were enfranchised, but their political capabilities and accumulation of political resources were severely truncated by the white-controlled political machines. Whereas in the postbellum South, the accumulation of political resources by the white working class increased its effective use of the political system in creating and reinforcing Jim Crow segregation, in the North, the European immigrants and their descendants (the groups most concerned about black encroachments on jobs and housing) exploited their control of the city political machines by gerrymandering ghetto neighborhoods. Thus they severely weakened the political participation, strength, and potential of the burgeoning black urban population.[44]

The social and economic consequences of this exclusion from urban politics is clearly revealed in the contrasting political experiences of those European immigrants who came to the United States in the late nineteenth and early twentieth centuries. Because they did not encounter the kind of racial-caste system imposed on black Americans, and because they arrived when urban political machines were not yet fully developed, those immigrant ethnics were able to penetrate discrimination barriers, to interact with the city power structures, and to shape their own political institutions.

The ethnic conflicts that characterized northern politics paradoxically contributed to the integration of the new arrivals into the urban areas. "The practical nature of the competition of the machine," observes Ira Katznelson, "acted to channel these conflicts into means of adjustment and acceptance; the new political linkages gave direction to social change. In this fashion, for instance, the Irish leaders of Tammany Hall brought Italians, Jews and Germans into decision-making positions in the Democratic party. . . . The very existence of the machines, throughout the North, depended on success in tapping fresh sources of support."[45]

For the immigrants, political mobility frequently translated into occupational and status mobility. For example, municipal contracts and other political favors were often directly related to the wealth accumulated by Irish immigrants in construction, in transport, and on the docks. It is of course true that not all immigrant groups enjoyed the same degree of success in machine politics; it is also true that in many situations, the significant gains of the political machines benefited only a few while not sufficiently addressing the needs of the masses. Despite such qualifications, "it is right to conclude that the political linkages the European immigrants fashioned before 1930 were significant. The machines were integrative mechanisms, and did provide power and socio-economic benefits to the communities they served. By 1930, significantly, as the black ghettos consolidated, the European immigrants' ghetto walls were crumbling."[46]

Although the increasing urbanization of black Americans provided them with the institutional differentiation and the social organization needed for efficacious political power, institutional discrimination severely depressed their political potential. Party machine organizations systematically excluded blacks from effective participation in the political process by such tactics as gerrymandering the boundaries of ghetto communities.

Although urban political leaders of both the Democratic and Republican parties needed and campaigned for black votes, they were not about to disturb the racial status quo by incorporating blacks into positions of power and influence within the city machines. This was not for them a realistic possibility because a great many white city-dwellers benefited economically, politically, and psychologically from black subordination and would have vigorously resisted efforts to allow Negroes some modicum of political control. Black participation in the machine was therefore channelled into parallel, powerless institutions. More specifically,

Negroes were linked to the party machines through what Katznelson has called city-wide "buffer institutions." These were
political organizations that had an independent line to the party
headquarters. They were not a formal part of the decentralized
structure of the city machine, and the flow of power was uni-
directional—from the party headquarters to the segregated black
institutions. Moreover, the machine hand-picked the middle-
class black leaders of these institutions and they could be promoted or removed from political positions as the machine saw
fit. Their primary obligation was to the white-controlled city
machines and they remained detached from and unresponsive
to the black masses. Commenting on the black leaders of these
segregated institutions, Katznelson states that:

> In the main, the black politicians, not selected by the
> group as a whole, and, in terms of class and status hardly
> typical of black migrants, sponsored substantively unre-
> sponsive programmes calculated to bring rewards to the
> leadership-elite. And even these unresponsive aims were not
> always achieved. . . . Given the critical structural decisions
> made by local white political elites, the choices open to
> black politicians were severely circumscribed. They were
> trapped in an emasculating cycle of limitations; given the
> unidirectional power limitations with which they were
> confronted, most black politicians of the period were un-
> derstandably (though I would argue, in retrospect, wrongly)
> convinced that only by accepting the institutionalized
> white-imposed limitations could they act effectively on be-
> half of their people.[47]

Because blacks were excluded from meaningful participation
in the white-controlled city machines, especially from World
War I through World War II, they were deprived of the kind of
political development experienced by white immigrant ethnics,
that is, what Martin Kilson has called the *politicization of ethnicity.* "This means simply to use ethnic patterns and prejudices as
the primary basis for interest-group and political formations, and
to build upon these to integrate a given ethnic community into
the wider politics of the city and the nation."[48]
Whereas the lower-class ethnics had received, through their
political machines, participatory incentives which enhanced their
political development, the black urban lower class, excluded

from this process, reached the beginning of the 1960s with little political participation, a high sense of powerlessness and estrangement from the institutionalized processes, and low political skill and knowledge. Moreover, because the Irish, Italian, Polish, and Jewish ethnic groups were fully incorporated into the city political machines, the middle-class segments of these groups were able to use their skills to organize their respective communities. Because the black middle class, on the other hand, was denied access to structural avenues for political participation, it could exert political influence only through the extrainstitutional civil rights movement. Martin Kilson has commented on this point:

> Civil rights politics was largely a middle-class affair: from 1915 to the 1950's the leadership and membership were mainly middle-class, and the large Negro lower strata had little political relationship to civil rights politics. This meant that the politics pursued by the Negro elites in most cities never produced a vertical integration of the elites with Negro lower strata. In short, the civil rights politics, which the neglect of the city machines caused Negro elites in most cities to adopt, had a class and status bias that prevented the black ghetto from taking on the attributes of an ethnic political subsystem—that is, an articulate and politically cohesive group within the structure of the city machine.[49]

What is interesting about black politics, however, is the emergence of lower-class black influence on political issues and decisions since the mid-1960s. Although this subject will be treated in greater detail in Chapter 6, some of the reasons for the shift from middle- to lower-class-oriented black politics will be outlined in the following section.

Industrial Growth and Changes in Black-White Interaction

In the foregoing analysis, I have attempted to show how the deterioration of race relations in the North at the turn of the century was traceable ultimately to basic social and demographic changes in American society. The changes in the systems of production in both the North and the South stimulated Negro migration from the southern rural areas to northern industrial centers and profoundly altered the quality and character of urban race relations. Just as the shift from a plantation economy to an industrializing economy transformed traditional patterns of race and class in the postbellum South, so too did industrial growth establish a new context for black-white interaction and confrontation in the North. The competitive form of race relations that emerged in the latter half of the industrial phase of race relations (the period from 1900 to the mid-twentieth century) shared many elements with the pattern of racial conflict that marred the postbellum period in the South. In both situations, racial conflicts between blacks and the white working class were inextricably linked to class conflicts among whites. However, there were also fundamental differences. The almost total subordination of blacks in the South was clearly related to the disintegration of the paternalistic bond between Negroes and the southern economic elite, because this disintegration cleared the path for what ultimately resulted in a united white segregation movement. Between 1880 and 1900, the position of southern blacks rapidly deteriorated, and they remained in a thoroughly subjugated state throughout the remaining period of industrial race relations. In the North, on the other hand, a united white movement against blacks never crystallized. In the first quarter of the twentieth century black entry into northern industry was based in part on the use by management of black workers as strikebreakers and as leverage against white workers' demands for higher wages and more fringe benefits. Management's concern about the rising labor costs and periodic labor shortages offset the normative pressures of racial exclusion. In this connection, then, the relationship between blacks and both working-class whites and the managers of industry seems to correspond more closely with the split labor-market theory of racial antagonism than with the orthodox Marxist explanations. In this particular period of race relations there is, in fact, little empirical support for the Marxist's contention that the capitalist class attempted to isolate the black labor force by imposing a system of racial stratification both in and outside of industries. Efforts to restrict black advancement in the latter phases of the industrial period of race relations were almost exclusively associated with the white working class. However, it could be argued that since employers attempted to cut costs by imposing discriminatory pay scales (in other words by developing a split labor market) the Marxist argument concerning management's effort to develop a white aristocracy is upheld. However, although the available data support the view that a wage differential did exist in many industries during this period, particularly in the South,[50] there is little indication that this represented management's efforts to divide the working class by developing a white labor aristocracy; rather the data suggest that management wanted to cut costs by allowing blacks to compete more or less freely in the open market and by discouraging black participation in labor unions. Accordingly, if the argument that business did want to encourage open competition between ethnic groups in the labor market is correct, then we would have to assume that in some situations northern employers were possibly under some duress not to hire blacks. For example, in his study of the steel workers, Brody points out that in 1917 "several steel firms in Pittsburgh hesitated to hire the [Negro] migrants" because "company officials feared the reaction of white employees."[51] Moreover, in some industries, aside from fearing sanctions by white laborers, employers still might have refused to hire cheaper black labor because of "a threatened loss of sales" from white patrons who resented the employment of blacks.[52] In some cases this resulted from a general anxiety about black encroachment; for example, the mere fact of seeing blacks in certain jobs might have been enough to generate concern among some whites who felt that blacks should be "kept in their place."[53] Nonetheless, we can only assume that the steady growth of blacks in industry during and following World War I, despite discriminatory practices in many firms, indicated that white workers had not developed sufficient resources in their struggles with management to impose segregation barriers in order to avoid being undercut by black labor in certain jobs. Indeed, industrialists' determination to hire black workers, irrespective of racial norms, was one of the main reasons why industry-wide unions such as the CIO reversed exclusionist racial policies and actively recruited black workers during the New Deal era. As long as blacks constituted a significant percentage of the unskilled and semiskilled labor force, and were nonunionized and available either as strikebreakers or as lower-paid labor, industry-wide unions were vulnerable to employer exploitation.[54] The efforts of industrial unions to organize blacks altered the context of confrontation and significantly reduced the racial tensions that had characterized the industrial sector during the early twentieth century.

But the changing position of blacks in the economic order represents only a partial picture of their experiences and adaptations to northern urban life. Residential segregation contributed to the growth of urban ghettoes. A housing shortage accompanied the rapid increase in the black urban population, and black "invasions" or ghetto "spillovers" into adjacent ethnic neighborhoods often produced racial flareups. The situation was especially problematic during and immediately following World War I, as racial animosity in the economic order reinforced and sometimes produced racial tension in the social order. Negroes encountered white resistance each time they encroached on areas where whites felt that they had prior claim, for example, residential communities, playgrounds, parks, and bathing beaches. The very fact that racial flareups in the early twentieth century were related to competition for jobs, housing, and recreational facilities indicated that whites were not always successful in institutionalizing mechanisms for social control. To the extent that the white masses did control blacks through systems of structured inequality (as in institutionalized segregation), racial conflict tended to be latent rather than manifest. This was most clearly demonstrated in the successful exclusion of blacks from meaningful participation in the urban political system. White ethnic control of the city machines was so complete throughout the first half of the twentieth century that blacks were never able to compete for municipal political rewards such as patronage jobs and government contracts and services.[55] Accordingly, the racial conflicts that permeated the economic and social orders never really penetrated the political sector.

Although northern blacks were unable to develop the degree of political power that white immigrants experienced during the first half of the twentieth century, they could not be completely ignored by politicians because they were free to vote. Historically, the ballot has been the main political resource of blacks.[56] However, prior to 1940, their votes generated only promises of token rewards from local, state, and national politicians, who feared political repercussions from whites, particularly lower-class white ethnics, if they became too responsive to black demands. It was not until the 1940s that the concentrated Negro vote in large cities became significant enough in pivotal northern states to determine close national elections.[57] And although national politicians limited their pursuit of race goals for fear of losing white supporters (Franklin D. Roosevelt sought to preserve or gain black support in 1940 by taking steps to increase Negro participation in the armed services, but he maintained segregated units), their racial policies became more progressive as the black vote increased in significance.[58]

Since the mid-twentieth century, the black vote has also become a crucial factor in the outcome of municipal elections in large urban centers. This increased voting power of urban blacks derives from changes in the racial composition of central cities. Washington, D.C., Newark, and Gary already have black majorities and cities such as Chicago, Cleveland, Philadelphia, St. Louis, and Detroit have approached a population composition which is one-third or more black. In Chicago, for example, the black population increased from one-seventh of the total population in 1950 to roughly one-third in 1972. This sharp rise in numbers has raised the specter of black control of cities and has provided a base for black politicians to run successfully not only for municipal political offices but also for state and national offices.[59]

In addition to the changing demographic structure of the city, the increase in urban black political power is related to the demise of the political machines. The movement of reform in government led to the decline and collapse of the powerful machines after 1940 and produced greater interparty competition, thereby increasing the importance of the black vote.[60] The existence of a powerful political machine usually meant that the opposing political party could be ignored, even when it attempted to lure black votes. In this connection, Bailey has observed that "the Negro politician's relative success in attaining race goals depends in part upon the extent of party strength among the general electorate and the amount of party control in the legislature. When the party is extremely strong in either or both cases, the Negro politician is less able to use his influence to effect civil rights policies; where the party is relatively weak, the Negro politician has a better chance."[61]

The demise of the political machines and the explosion in the size of the black population paved the way for a new pattern of urban politics that clearly emerged in the 1960s. Whereas the civil rights politics of black elites in previous years had little relationship to the specific problems of the ghetto masses, the new black politics is intimately associated with the human struggles in the ghetto. The increased politicization of the black lower class, in the aftermath of the riots and black protest movement in the 1960s, impelled the black middle-class politicians to articulate, in a more forceful manner, the particular needs and interests of their ghetto constituencies.[62]

At the very time that blacks are gaining political control in cities across the nation, however, the concentration of power in metropolitan areas has shifted away from political parties. Fundamental economic and social changes of modern industrial society have created a new center of power in the form of complex corporate bureaucracies that have little connection with municipal political structures but that do have enormous control of the economic and social resources of the city. The implications of this shift in power for urban areas in general and the black population in particular are explored in the following chapter.

5 MODERN INDUSTRIALIZATION AND THE ALTERATION OF COMPETITIVE RACE RELATIONS

A discussion of overt black-white tensions in the stage of industrial race relations must invariably refer to the labor-market strife generated by black encroachment in various branches of industry; it must refer to racial antagonism in the industrial order. However, in the period of modern industrialization, the very basis for severe racial strife in the industrial sector has been eroded not only by economic changes but also by political changes designed to mediate or resolve class and racial conflicts grounded in the social relations of production. But, as we shall see in this chapter, these economic and political changes have not significantly alleviated racial tensions in American society. Instead they have produced and facilitated a shift in racial conflict away from the industrial order to the sociopolitical order, a shift which has also increased the importance of economic class position, thereby decreasing the importance of race in determining the extent to which individual blacks have access to or are able to develop resources deemed important for life chances and survival.

The Increase in Black Unemployment

Few people would disagree with the assertion that, as blacks in America became more urbanized, they were increasingly able to improve their general economic situation. Prior to 1910, Negroes had been denied entry into even the most menial jobs in the manufacturing sector; but, beginning with the World War I period and throughout the 1920s, they could at least procure unskilled jobs in the growing automobile and steel industries. However, the real breakthrough occurred during World War II, when President Roosevelt's executive order banned discrimination in defense plants and in government agencies, when an acute nationwide labor shortage existed, and when the government subsidized training programs. All these factors enabled blacks to move into primarily semiskilled jobs in manufacturing—jobs in which they had not been concentrated previously. In fact, they even made entry into some white-collar jobs, particularly clerical positions with municipal, state, and federal government agencies.

Although some blacks lost jobs following World War II, because of cutbacks in defense industries and the reentry of white veterans into the civilian labor force, the continual expansion of the economy following the war, partly because of successful government attempts to avoid a postwar recession, created a relatively favorable job market for black workers. Indeed, the steady stream of black migrants from the rural South was absorbed into the urban labor market throughout the 1940s and early 1950s. However, after 1954 it became clear that serious and chronic labor-market problems were affecting a large segment of the black population.

Although labor economists have frequently noted the limitations of official employment rates as an indicator of a group's economic well-being, nonetheless these rates "have come to be generally accepted as the most significant single measure of relative disadvantage."[1] It is therefore important to note that the two-to-one unemployment ratio between blacks and whites since 1954 has shown very little change, despite shifts from good to bad economic years since then (see table 5). Blacks actually fared better in relation to white unemployment prior to 1950. A black/white unemployment ratio of 0.90 was reported in the 1930 federal census report, and one of 1.18 in the 1940 report.[2] In 1948 and 1949, the first two years that official annual employment statistics were recorded, the rates were 1.68 and 1.59 respectively.

If unemployment has become a chronic problem for the black population generally, it is reaching disastrous proportions for young blacks in the labor force. In 1954, the black teenage unemployment percentage was only slightly greater than that for whites. However, each year since 1966 a greater than two-to-one black-white teenage unemployment ratio has been officially recorded. From 1970 to 1974, black teenagers' unemployment has averaged 32 percent, and the 1974 rate of 32.9 percent was close to two and a half times greater than the recorded white teenagers' unemployment (see table 6).[3] At the time of this writing, the most recent official labor statistics indicate that for June of 1976 the unemployment percentage for black teenagers jumped

TABLE 5. Unemployment Rates by Race for Persons Sixteen Years and Over, 1948–1974

	Unemployment Rate		
Year	Black and Other Races*	White	Ratio of Black and Other Races to White
1948	5.9%	3.5%	1.69
1949	8.9	5.6	1.59
1950	9.0	4.9	1.84
1951	5.3	3.1	1.71
1952	5.4	2.8	1.93
1953	4.5	2.7	1.67
1954	9.9	5.0	1.98
1955	8.7	3.9	2.23
1956	8.3	3.6	2.30
1957	7.9	3.8	2.07
1958	12.6	6.1	2.07
1959	10.7	4.8	2.33
1960	10.2	4.9	2.08
1961	12.4	6.0	2.07
1962	10.9	4.9	2.22
1963	10.8	5.0	2.16
1964	9.6	4.6	2.09
1965	8.1	4.1	1.98
1966	7.3	3.3	2.21
1967	7.4	3.4	2.17
1968	6.7	3.2	2.09
1969	6.4	3.1	2.06
1970	8.2	4.5	1.82
1971	9.9	5.4	1.83
1972	10.0	5.0	2.00
1973	8.9	4.3	2.07
1974	9.9	5.0	1.98

Source: U.S. Bureau of the Census, "The Social and Economic Status of the Black Population in the United States, 1974," *Current Population Reports,* Series P-23, no. 48 (Washington, D.C.: Government Printing Office, 1975).

Note: The unemployment rate is the percentage of the civilian labor force that is unemployed.

*"Black and other races" is a United States Census Bureau designation, and is used in those cases where data are not available solely for blacks. However, because about 90 percent of the population designated by "Black and other races" is black, statistics reported for this category generally reflect the condition of the black population.

TABLE 6. Unemployment Rates by Race for Persons Sixteen to Nineteen Years Old, 1954–1974

| Year | Unemployment Rate | | Ratio of Black and Other Races to White |
	Black and Other Races	White	
1954	16.5%	12.1%	1.37
1955	15.8	10.3	1.53
1956	18.2	10.2	1.78
1957	19.1	10.6	1.80
1958	27.4	14.4	1.90
1959	26.1	13.1	1.99
1960	24.4	13.4	1.82
1961	27.6	15.3	1.80
1962	25.1	13.3	1.89
1963	30.4	15.5	1.96
1964	27.2	14.8	1.84
1965	26.2	13.4	1.96
1966	25.4	11.2	2.26
1967	26.5	11.0	2.41
1968	25.0	11.0	2.27
1969	24.0	10.7	2.24
1970	29.1	13.5	2.16
1971	31.7	15.1	2.10
1972	33.5	14.2	2.36
1973	30.2	12.6	2.37
1974	32.9	14.0	2.35

Source: U.S. Department of Labor, *Handbook of Labor Statistics* (Washington, D.C.: Government Printing Office, 1975).

to 40.3 while the increase for white teenagers was quite small (to 16.0).[4]

The high rates of unemployment for black teenagers in the 1970s are to some extent related to the general slowdown in the American economy. However, even in the relatively high business activity year of 1969, the rate of unemployment for black teenagers was 24 percent.[5] Moreover, in 1974, the percentage of unemployment for black teenagers was almost five times as high as that for black adults (whose rate of 7.5 nearly doubled the white adult rate of 4.2), whereas twenty years earlier black teenagers had been unemployed at a rate (16.5) only slightly less than twice the black adult rate (9.4).[6] Yet even the very high official unemployment figures do not capture the real condition of black teenage joblessness. A 1971 study conducted by the United States Department of Labor showed that while the black teenage unemployment rate increased by ten percentage points from the first quarter of 1970 to the second quarter of 1971, their rate of participation in the labor force declined by more than seven points (from 51.2 to 43.8 percent).[7] These figures suggest that the higher the unemployment, the more that black teenagers give up looking for work altogether.

The sharp rise in the black teenage population is one of the factors that has contributed to its joblessness.[8] The number of central-city black youths aged sixteen to nineteen increased by almost 75 percent in less than a decade (1960 to 1969), compared with an increase of only 14 percent for white teenagers of the same ages. Furthermore, black young adults (aged twenty to twenty-four) increased in number by two-thirds, three times the population increase for their white counterparts.[9] It is, then, nearly an understatement to say that the increase of younger blacks in the central city constitutes a population explosion.[10] It hardly needs emphasizing that what observers call the "central city crisis" derives in part from the unprecedented increase in younger blacks, many of whom are not enrolled in school, are jobless, and are a source of delinquency, crime, and unrest in the ghettoes.[11] This population explosion of young blacks has occurred at the very time when structural changes in the economy pose serious problems for unskilled Negroes in and out of the labor force.

The Effect of Structural Changes in the Economy on Central-City Employment

Following World War II, fundamental technological and economic changes facilitated the increasing decentralization of American businesses. Improvements in transportation and communication have made the use of open and relatively inexpensive tracts of land outside central cities more feasible not only for manufacturing, wholesaling, and retailing but also for residential development. The traditional central-city multistory factories have been rendered obsolete with the introduction and diffusion of single-level assembly line modes of production. Concurrent with the growing cost and limited availability of land, tax rates rose, traffic congestion increased, and vandalism and other crimes that multiplied the operating costs of city industries mounted; many firms, previously restricted to the central-city locations near ports, freight terminals, and passenger facilities, began to rely more heavily on truck transportation and to locate in outlying sites near interchanges, the expanding metropolitan expressway system, and new housing construction. Moreover, the use of the automobile has freed firms from the necessity of locating near mass transportation facilities in order to attract a labor force. Consequently, industry savings in transportation and communication are no longer necessarily associated with central-city locations. Indeed, in the nation's twelve largest metropolitan areas, the central city's proportion of all manufacturing employment dropped from 66.1 percent in 1947 to less than 40 percent in 1970.[12]

This remarkable shift in industry concentration has occurred despite the fact that only a relatively small number of businesses have actually moved to the suburbs.[13] The problem for the central city is not so much the loss of industry as it is the lack of industrial growth or expansion. Manufacturing employment has tended to expand outside central cities, especially in the new aircraft, aerospace, and electronics industries. In a recent study of ten large metropolitan areas, 79 percent of the employment growth in manufacturing from 1959 to 1967 occurred outside the central city (see table 7). Furthermore, the growth of retail and wholesale trade was overwhelmingly located in the suburbs.

While the economic stalemate in the central-city manufacturing sector has meant limited opportunities for those seeking better paying blue-collar jobs, the developing service-producing industries have effected a rapid expansion of white-collar employment; in the last three decades the national economic structure has actually shifted gradually from a basis in goods-producing industries (manufacturing, construction, mining, and agriculture) to a concentration on service-producing industries (transportation, service, government, public utilities, trade, and finance). In 1947, the majority (51 percent) of American workers were located in the goods-producing sector of the economy; by 1968, 64 percent of American workers were employed in the service-producing industries, and by 1980 that figure will increase to 68 percent.[14] The nationwide shift from goods to services has been most pronounced in the central cities. Furthermore, the expanding employment opportunities in the clerical, professional, and administrative positions associated with finance, insurance, and real estate firms, professional and business services, and federal,

TABLE 7. Employment outside the Central City in Ten Large Metropolitan Areas by Industry, 1959 and 1967

Area and Industry	% of SMSA Employment outside Central City*		% of SMSA Employment Growth outside Central City, 1959 to 1967
	1959	1967	
Average, 10 areas	28	32	54
Atlanta	22	27	36
Baltimore	30	37	72
Boston	61	62	73
Houston	7	6	5
Kansas City	26	28	37
New Orleans	18	24	40
New York	15	19	49
Philadelphia	40	46	79
St. Louis	42	49	85
Washington, D.C.	39	49	70
Average, all industries	28	32	54
Manufacturing	37	41	79
Retail trade	32	41	78
Wholesale trade	16	22	68
Services	23	29	42
Finance, insurance, and real estate	13	18	42
Other	27	28	31

Source: U.S. Department of Labor, *Manpower Report of the President* (Washington, D.C.: Government Printing Office, 1971).
*The standard metropolitan statistical area (SMSA) in each case is that for which the central-city was substantially the same as the central city county. To ensure comparability the definition for each area for 1959 was corrected to 1967 boundaries. Government workers and the self-employed are excluded.

state, and local government agencies have higher educational and training requirements than those associated with blue-collar employment (except possibly for the skilled crafts).[15] It is true that the service industries that employ low-skilled workers (in jobs ranging from hospital orderly to dishwasher) have also seen considerable growth. But, such jobs are poorly paid, menial, and dead-end. Accordingly, both the lack of job expansion in the manufacturing sector and the fact that desirable jobs in the service industries require education and training mean that the better paid and more desirable positions into which workers can enter without special skills and/or higher education are decreasing in central cities not only in relative terms but sometimes in absolute numbers.[16] I would like to explore this point one step further.

In one interpretation of the relationship between joblessness and structural changes in the economy, Charles C. Killingsworth maintains that a "twist" in the demand for different types of labor has occurred in recent years.[17] More specifically, there has been a long-run decline in the demand for low-skilled, poorly educated workers and a long-run rise in the demand for high-skilled, well-educated workers; and that this twist has "proceeded farther and faster than adjustments in the supply of labor, resulting in a growing imbalance in the labor market."[18] From this, Killingsworth concluded that "the declining participation rates among the less educated must reflect in some measure a form of 'hidden unemployment'—that is, workers who had abandoned an active search for work because of discouragement, but who were nevertheless willing and able to work."[19] One certainly does not need a great deal of imagination to see the relevance of this argument for the black population, particularly in view of their disproportionately high representation in the category of low-skilled and poorly educated workers and in the increasing number of discouraged workers who have given up actively seeking work (the Department of Labor reports that "among persons not in the labor force in early 1975, 4.4 percent of the black and other races and 1.6 percent of whites were discouraged workers").[20]

Another interpretation of the labor-market problems of blacks, especially with respect to the central city, an interpretation consistent with my analysis in the preceding paragraphs, suggests that the problem is not one of a declining number of available jobs but a decrease in the opportunity to obtain stable higher-paying jobs. In this vein, Doeringer and Piore report that "in many cities it appears that those employment and income problems do not reflect absolute barriers to employment so much as a deficiency of high rate or otherwise preferred employment opportunities. For example, a study of the low-wage labor market in Boston showed that employment in hospitals, hotels, warehouses, building maintenance services, industrial sweatshops, and so forth, is readily available to the disadvantaged. But attractive high wage employment—jobs which constitute, in the current language of manpower, 'meaningful employment opportunities'—were much less accessible."[21] The observation relates explicitly to yet another aspect of the structural shifts in the economy, an aspect that has developed hand in hand with the decentralization of industry and the movement from goods to services and that has brought the problems of black employment into even sharper relief—the development of quite distinct labor markets in advanced industrial America, a subject to which I now turn.[22]

The Growth of Corporate Industries and the Surplus Black Labor Force

The high jobless rate among a substantial segment of the black population is partly related to the rapid growth of corporate industries. Representing the very center of the new American economy, corporate industries are characterized by vertically integrated production processes and technologically progressive systems of production and distribution. The growth of production depends more on technical progress and increases in physical capital per worker than on the growth of employment. Firms in the corporate sector have either national or international markets, and they range from a variety of goods-producing industries (that develop on a large scale such products as aluminum, oil, copper, steel, electrical equipment, appliances, automobiles, and various foods and soaps) to service-producing industries such as transportation firms (airlines, branches of shipping and railroads), public utilities (natural gas, telephone, and electric), finance firms (banking and investment), and wholesale trade. Jobs in the corporate industries are distinguished by stable employment, high wages (that are often pegged to cost-of-living and productivity increases), favorable working conditions, advancement opportunities, and due process and equity in the administration of work rules.[23] Because the industrial structure of corporate industries is relatively stable, production and employment are regularized to prevent losses stemming from unused productive capacity, planning is instituted to stabilize prices and control demand for goods, the demand for labor is inelastic, and work is stabilized on a year-round, full-time basis. For all these reasons, labor unions have been able to thrive in corporate industries.

The growth of the corporate sector has resulted in the expansion of industrial technology and thereby in an increase in the number of workers victimized by technological unemployment. The expansion of industrial technology has sharply increased the productive capacity or output per man-hour while, at the same time, decreasing the need for semiskilled or unskilled labor. Moreover, since production capacity has tended to increase much more rapidly than purchasing power, corporate industries have preferred, in some situations, to reduce production to maintain the high profit-margins, thereby eliminating the need to increase employment or create new jobs. In short, an increasing number of corporate sector workers have become redundant because the demand for labor is decreased in the short run by the growth of technology and in the long run by the gap between productivity and the demand for goods. In the face of the decreasing demand for labor and the more rigorous prerequisites for higher levels of employment, teenagers and other workers entering the labor market for the first time find it increasingly difficult to obtain employment in the corporate sector. Blacks constitute a sizable percentage of both corporate sector workers who have become redundant because of advancing technology and the new job-seekers locked out of this sector of the economy.[24] This point requires amplification.

Recent research on unemployment in thirty of the nation's largest cities revealed that blacks do not experience employment barriers in low-paid, menial, and casual jobs but rather in the more desirable, higher-paying jobs in the large manufacturing, wholesale trade, construction, and finance industries, representative industries of the corporate sector.[25] In fact, the greater the proportion of city jobs found in these industries, the higher the black unemployment rate.[26] If corporate industries are associated with a surplus black labor force, it is necessary to consider, in addition to technological unemployment and employment barriers pertaining to education and training, the relationship between labor unions and blue-collar employment.

Unions in the corporate sector tend to be dominated by an elite labor force which, through effective organization, has solidified its hold on the higher-paying and respectable blue-collar jobs. Moreover, this labor force has successfully pressed for consistent wage hikes, increased fringe benefits, and has generated a protective welfare system financed in part by management. The net effect is the virtual elimination of the employability of a floating, transient labor force. Employers who hire additional workers in high-demand periods find themselves penalized because of changes in compensation and work rules promoted by trade unions and supplemented by legislation. Thus, employer expenditures for unemployment insurance, social security, workmen's compensation insurance, and other fringe benefits have made labor costs more a function of the number of workers employed than of the number of hours worked. In many instances corporate management finds it cheaper to simply pay their regular work force overtime than to hire additional employees under the welfare umbrella; consequently, even when demand is high, transient workers are forced to remain in the low-wage sector or to join the ranks of the unemployed. Meanwhile, in the face of continuing automation, the labor unions seek to preserve the interests of the nuclear work force by supporting a policy that gradually reduces the number of less senior workers when demand is low, thereby increasing the transient work force. In short, the pattern of overemployment for senior workers reinforces the pattern of unemployment for junior or transient workers in the higher-paying corporate industries of the United States economy.[27]

These corporate industry employment patterns have all but eliminated the importance of race in labor-management strife. In the past, management exacerbated tensions between white and black workers by creating a split labor market—split in the sense that black labor was considered cheaper than white labor, regardless of the work involved.[28] As I indicated in the previous chapter, these tensions often erupted into violence when blacks were used as strikebreakers to undercut white workers. However, although the split labor-market thesis seems to have had considerable relevance in the industrial period of race relations, especially in the last quarter of the nineteenth century and the first quarter of the twentieth century, it is not very applicable to corporate industries today. This is not to suggest that the elite white labor force is no longer concerned about being undercut by black workers, but that, because of both the growth of powerful unions following passage of protective union legislation in the New Deal era and the nationwide equal employment legislation of the 1950s and 1960s (including the Federal Civil Rights Law of 1964), employers are no longer able to undercut the white labor force by hiring cheaper black labor. Prior to the passage of both protective union legislation and equal employment legislation, employers had little hesitation in hiring nonunionized blacks with qualifications or abilities similar to those of workers in order to cut costs. Moreover, in situations where white workers had sufficient power to resist the hiring of blacks at either similar skill-levels, higher skill-levels, or at supervisory levels, management often employed blacks in jobs below their skill level or established segregated work forces with depressed wages. Today, however, in the face of law stipulating equal pay for equal work, there is no economic incentive to hire cheap black labor. Accordingly, the problems blacks are now facing in finding desirable blue-collar jobs in corporate industries have more to do with difficulties in being hired than with discrimination in pay scales.[29]

However, if the black lower class is experiencing decreasing opportunities for higher-wage employment, the black middle class is enjoying unprecedented success in finding white-collar jobs in both the corporate sector and the growing government sector.

The Expansion of the Corporate and Government Sectors and the Growth of the Black Middle Class

The structure of the labor market as far as lower-class blacks are concerned has not been significantly altered despite the programs of affirmative action established by the Office of Federal

Contract Compliance (OFCC). Affirmative action programs have had little impact in situations where labor supply is greater than labor demand (this is the case with the higher-paying blue-collar jobs of the corporate sector in which employment opportunities for lesser-trained and experienced blacks have significantly decreased due to the increase of labor-saving technology and the effective efforts of unions in protecting the remaining jobs for the nuclear work force).[30]

On the other hand, affirmative action programs have benefited those blacks who are able to qualify for the expanding white-collar salaried positions in the corporate sector, positions that have higher educational and training requirements than those associated with blue-collar employment (except possibly for the skilled crafts).[31] And the more training and education a given white-collar position requires, the less likely that the labor supply will exceed the labor demand. It is no coincidence therefore that the corporate industries which first initiated affirmative action programs were the ones that had the greatest need for trained and educated manpower because of growth or expansion. As early as 1964, Tom Kahn reported that the rapidly expanding industries such as IBM, American Telephone and Telegraph, Lockheed, Goodyear, Western Electric, Radio Corporation of America, and Texas Instruments (electronics) regularly visited black colleges to recruit mathematicians, sales and managerial trainees, engineers, and scientists.[32] Since 1965, the combination of the increasing demand for white-collar salaried employees and the governmental pressures for demonstrated affirmative action programs has generated major efforts on the part of corporations to recruit and hire talented and educated blacks. In this connection, Richard Freeman has stated that "federally required programs of affirmative action, involving job quotas that favor minorities, have made minority hiring an explicit goal of major corporations. At I.B.M., for example, every manager is told that his annual performance evaluation—on which promotions, raises and bonuses critically depend—includes a report on his success in meeting affirmative action goals."[33]

The efforts of corporations to recruit college-trained blacks increased sharply between 1965 and 1970, as revealed in table 8. The figures reported are indeed striking, indicating that the average number of recruitment visits of representatives of corporations to predominantly black colleges increased from 4 in 1960 to 50 in 1965 and then jumped to 297 in 1970. And schools such as Atlanta University and Southern University, to which no visits were made in 1960, received respectively 510 and 600 corporate representatives in 1970. However, Freeman informs us that: "Between 1970 and 1975 the number of recruiters visiting black colleges did . . . fall as the college job market worsened. A sample of 10 schools surveyed by mail in 1975 reported a drop in the average number of recruiters from 309 per school in 1970 to 240

TABLE 8. Recruitment Visits of Representatives of Corporations to Predominantly Black Colleges and Universities

College	Number of Representatives of Corporations Interviewing Job Candidates		
	1960	1965	1970
Atlanta University	0	160	510
Howard	*	100	619
Clark	0	40	350
Alabama A&M	0	0	100
Alabama State	0	7	30
Hampton	20	247	573
Jackson State	*	*	280
Johnson C. Smith	0	25	175
Morehouse	*	*	300
Miles	0	12	54
Norfolk State	5	100	250
North Carolina A&T	6	80	517
Prairie View	*	*	350
Southern	0	25	600
Suno	0	5	75
Texas Southern	0	69	175
Tuskegee	50	85	404
Virginia State	0	25	325
Winston-Salem	*	*	25
Virginia Union University	5	25	150
Xavier	0	44	185
Average per school	4	50	297

Source: Richard Freeman, "The Implications of the Changing Labor Market for Members of Minority Groups," in Margaret G. Gordon, ed., *Higher Education and the Labor Market*, © copyright 1973 by McGraw-Hill. Used with permission.
*Not available.

in 1975. This decline of 22% matched that for MIT over the period 1970–1974 . . . which suggests that recruiting fell off at the black colleges at about the same pace as elsewhere. From these data and the records of those hired by national corporations, it becomes clear that for the first time the national professional-managerial job market was open to blacks."[34] The vigorous recruitment of the best black talent by corporations is probably one of the reasons why the proportion of black male workers in white-collar positions increased from 16 to 24 percent from 1964 to 1974 with the bulk of this increase occurring in the higher-level professional, technical, and administrative positions (the proportion of white males in white-collar positions remained slightly over 40 percent during this period).[35] However there is yet another, and probably more important, reason for the increased proportion of black workers in white-collar positions— the growth of the government sector.

In recent years, greater and greater pressure has been placed on the state to provide services so that workers having employment difficulties can at least maintain their living standard. The pressures for state intervention are based not only on the consequences of the growth of the surplus labor force, for example, increased unemployment, but also on the problem of chronic inflation. Indeed, the existence of what economists call stagflation, that is, persistent high rates of unemployment and chronic inflation, has become a characteristic feature of modern industrial societies and has placed severe strains on the basic functions of the welfare state.[36] Frequently unable to gain employment in either the corporate sector or the government sector, unemployed and employed workers of the low-wage industries have become more and more dependent on the government to meet their needs through various welfare programs, including welfare benefits, emergency and general assistance benefits, medicaid and medicare, food stamps and commodity distribution, supplementary education programs and public housing.[37]

One effect of the increased welfare expenditures has been an expansion of the government bureaucracies that administer these programs. The government sector has also grown in recent years as a consequence of the spread of more general welfare requirements (social security, veterans programs, and community development) and of the proliferation of responsibilities associated with defense, the regulation of commerce and industry, and so on. Indeed, the percentage of workers in the government sector has increased from 12.1 in 1960 to 16.1 in 1970 (see table 9).

TABLE 9. Employed Workers by Sector and Race, 1960 and 1970

	Total Nos.	Private Sector		Government Sector	
		No.	%	No.	%
1960					
White	58,023,795	51,055,702	88.0	6,968,093	12.0
Black	6,622,768	5,743,064	86.7	879,704	13.3
All Workers	64,646,563	56,798,766	87.9	7,847,797	12.1
1970					
White	69,402,115	58,594,922	84.4	10,807,193	15.6
Black	7,403,056	5,822,390	78.6	1,580,666	21.4
All Workers	76,805,171	64,417,312	83.9	12,387,854	16.1

Source: U.S. Bureau of the Census, *Census of the Population*, 1960 and 1970, Subject Reports, Occupational Characteristics.

Although the expansion of the government sector has in part meant that more and more workers have become dependent on the state to satisfy their basic needs, and a disproportionate percentage of these workers are black, it has also meant that a greater percentage of higher-paying jobs (wages and salaries are relatively high because most government services require a trained or skilled labor force) are available to the black middle class.[38] For example, in 1960, 13.3 percent of the total employed black labor force worked in the government sector; by 1970, that figure had increased to 21.4 percent (see table 9). And from May 1973 to May 1974, 64 percent of all new federal employees came from minority groups.

The increase in higher-paying job opportunities for qualified blacks through the expansion of the government sector has had little significance for the occupational advancement of the black underclass. The educational and/or training prerequisites for most of the white-collar positions (and even for the blue-collar positions under government contract, for example, in construction) serve to effectively screen out poorly trained blacks who are subsequently forced to accept employment in the low-wage sector of mostly noncorporate industries. This is true despite the rising levels of secondary education for black workers concentrated in the low-wage sector.

Lower-Class Blacks and the Low-Wage Sector

The problems of labor-market segmentation for lesser-trained blacks are dramatically revealed when the rising levels of education among workers in the low-wage sector are considered. Although educational levels have increased throughout the population (the percentage of blacks aged twenty to twenty-four who have completed high school increased from 42 in 1960 to 72 in 1974),[39] the largest jump in median education associated with occupations has occurred in the lower-paying operative, laborer, and service-worker jobs. From 1952 to 1972, the median educational level for workers in these positions increased by 27, 35, and 36 percent respectively; the increase for professional and technical workers was less than 1 percent and it was only 6 percent for managers and administrators (see table 10). We can infer that these changes are particularly problematic for the black population in central cities. In 1970, three out of every five black men employed in the central cities were in comparatively low-level job categories of nonfarm laborers, service workers, and operatives, as opposed to only one out of every

TABLE 10. Education by Occupational Level, 1952–1972

	Median Education in Years		
Occupational Level	1952	1972	% Increase
Professional, techni- cal workers	16+	16.3	0–1
Managers and admini- strators	12.2	12.9	6
Farmers and farm workers	8.3	9.4	13
Sales workers	12.3	12.7	3
Clerical workers	12.5	12.6	0–1
Craftsmen and similar	10.1	12.2	21
Operatives	9.1	11.6	27
Nonfarm laborers	8.3	11.2	35
Service workers	8.8	12.0	36

Source: U.S. Department of Labor, *Manpower Report of the President*, (Washington, D.C.: Government Printing Office, 1973).

three white males. Moreover, almost three out of every five black women were in service or operative jobs, which was twice the rate for white women.[40] Although some of the jobs included in these aggregate statistics are probably part of the high-wage corporate or government sectors (particularly the operative positions, which tend to be among the higher-paying semiskilled jobs usually associated with the manufacturing industries), the statistics provide a rough estimate of the heavy concentration of blacks in the low-wage labor force of central cities. They also underscore both the present employment difficulties experienced by black workers with only a high school education or less and their high unemployment rate. (As revealed in table 11,

TABLE 11. Unemployment Rates by Educational Attainment, Both Sexes, 1974 and 1975, Age 18+

	Years of School	Total % Unemployed	% White	% Nonwhite	% GAP (NW=W)
1974	Less than 12	6.7	6.1	9.3	3.2
	12	4.7	4.3	8.9	4.6
	More than 12	3.1	2.9	5.3	2.4
1975	Less than 12	12.6	11.7	17.0	5.3
	12	9.1	8.4	15.0	6.6
	More than 12	4.9	4.7	7.2	2.5

Source: Congress of the United States, *The Unemployment of Nonwhite Americans: The Effects of Alternative Policies,* Background Paper No. 11 (Washington, D.C.: Congressional Budget Office, July 19, 1976).

the less educated workers—both nonwhites and whites—had higher unemployment rates than the more educated workers during the recession period of 1974–75. The white and nonwhite unemployment gap is substantially larger for those workers who have not had some postsecondary education than for those who have had training beyond high school.)

The high unemployment rates in the central-city ghettoes are directly related to high labor turnover rates in the low-wage or secondary labor market. Recent data on employer's and workers' attitudes clearly indicate the instability of the low-wage labor market.

Employers complain of lateness, absenteeism and turnover among workers. Workers are especially bitter about arbitrary management, low wages and job insecurity. As these comments suggest, the instability appears to be characteristic of both jobs and workers. Certain of the jobs available to the disadvantaged—jobs in hospitals and hotels for example—although menial and low paying, are stable, but turnover among the employees who hold them is relatively high. Other jobs—in non-union construction, seasonal manufacturing and the like—are very unstable and are not organized to provide continuous employment. Whatever its cause, however, the amount of job changing which occurs means that any given level of employment in the secondary sector is associated with a higher level of frictional unemployment than in the primary sector. In a sense, therefore, high levels of turnover and frictional unemployment may be taken as the salient characteristic of the secondary market.[41]

High rates of unemployment in black ghettoes serve to preserve and reinforce the low-wage labor force. To repeat, because of the legions of unemployed black workers, particularly those under twenty-one, wages are kept low and employers are able to replace workers at any time. Moreover, lack of union organization provides little insulation against the supply-and-demand pressures in the labor market, thereby further depressing wages.[42] Jobs in the low-wage sector, particularly in urban areas where most blacks are concentrated, have a considerably lower percentage of white workers and a substantially higher percentage of black workers than jobs in the corporate and government sectors. Indeed, many low-wage sector jobs have come to be identified with the lower-class nonwhite urban labor force. It is not surprising therefore that recent studies of unemployment in the urban core reveal that blacks do not experience any special employment barriers in the casual, low-paid, and menial jobs of the low-wage sector.[43] In fact, many of these jobs remain unfilled despite the extremely high unemployment rate of blacks in the inner city. Employers constantly complain of the difficulty of attracting and keeping a stable work force and often comment that some blacks seem to be more willing to go on welfare than to accept available work.

However, the situation for inner-city black workers is far more complicated than such observations suggest. Research on black employment problems has consistently shown that poor blacks tend not only to value work but also to feel that self-respect and employment are inseparable. Enduring lack of success in the labor market lowers their self-confidence and promotes feelings of resignation that can lead to abandoning the job-search temporarily, if not permanently.[44] Nowhere is this more clearly demonstrated than in Elliot Liebow's sensitive study of streetcorner men in a Washington, D.C., ghetto. "The most important fact is that a man who is able and willing to work cannot earn enough money to support himself, his wife, and one or more children," states Liebow. "A man's chances for working regularly are good only if he is willing to work for less than he can live on, and sometimes not even then. On some jobs, the wage rate is deceptively higher than on others, but the higher the wage rate, the more difficult it is to get the job, and the less the job security."[45]

Liebow's research demonstrates that the attitude of lower-status black males toward low-paying and menial jobs is a reflection of the general societal attitude toward those jobs. The jobs filled by low-status inner-city blacks tend to be underpaid, uninteresting, dirty, and hard; they do not provide respect, status, opportunity, or advancement; therefore, it is not surprising that, like the rest of society, the low-status black male disdainfully views such employment. "He cannot do otherwise," states Liebow. "He cannot draw from a job those values which other people do not put into it."[46]

Liebow's research was conducted in the early sixties. Since then, as the foregoing discussion has shown, the job-market situation for residents in ghetto communities has actually deteriorated. In the Oakland community of Chicago's South Side, for instance, 32 percent of the neighborhood's 4,323 work force was unemployed in early 1976. "Times are hard," an unemployed worker on the South Side observed, "You go in for a job interview and they tell you they can give you $2.00 an hour. Now, what can you do with $80.00 a week these days? But, when you say you want more money, they say you don't want to work."[47]

It is no doubt true that in recent years, attitudes concerning low-status work have changed. Workers today are less willing to accept the kinds of low-paying and menial jobs that their grandfathers or fathers readily accepted. To some extent, this change in attitude is related to a revolution of rising expectations, not only for the black poor, but for all citizens of America—expectations generated by economic progress and by the democratic welfare state's official recognition of human suffering.[48] Moreover, many of the black poor have internalized the values emanating from the civil rights and black protest movements, values which promote black pride, and explicitly reject the view that disadvantaged minorities should be content with a system of unequal rewards. Furthermore, unlike his father or grandfather, the low-status dishwasher, hospital orderly, or janitor need not attach himself permanently to a specific job. There are other low-status jobs available, and there are alternative income sources in welfare and in illegal activities which, in combination with attitudes disdaining low-status work, contribute to the instability of the low-wage work force. Peter B. Doeringer's empirical study of the ABCD Federal Manpower Project in Boston reports that workers, when asked why they quit ABCD jobs, "mentioned the low wages, the poor working conditions and the lack of advancement opportunities. These workers know that menial jobs are always available and that the accumulation of an erratic work history would not be a barrier to obtaining menial jobs in the future."[49]

The underclass also knows that illegal activities, in many respects, provide a more lucrative alternative to low-wage employment. It was estimated in a recent study that roughly 20 percent of the adult residents in Harlem lived entirely on illegal income in 1966.[50] This same study also reported the results of intensive interviews with twenty-eight black youths, aged eighteen to twenty-four, many of whom regarded illegitimate hustling activities (numbers, gambling, narcotic sales, prostitution) as an easier, more desirable mechanism for achieving status and success in their neighborhoods than pursuing legitimate but low-level employment.[51]

Finally, welfare provides another substitute for low-wage and menial employment. Recent data on public assistance in six of the largest northern metropolitan areas in the United States indicate that, contrary to conventional beliefs, "The rapid rise that occurred during the 1960's in the number of persons on welfare resulted mainly from an increase in the number of urban nonmigrants applying for welfare."[52] Blacks born in the North were more likely to adopt the welfare alternative than blacks born in the South. This was true despite the fact that the level of education of northern-born blacks was higher than the level of education of southern-born blacks. Moreover, "the migrants (both men and women) have tended to have higher labor force participation rates and lower unemployment rates than black natives in the cities in question."[53] Data such as these have to be interpreted cautiously, however, because the lower welfare and unemployment rates and the higher labor-force participation rates of the southern migrants may be partly related to the fact that many southern-born blacks who would be likely candidates for the unemployment and welfare roles simply return to the South if they are unsuccessful in finding work, and that the migrants who remain tend to be those who have experienced greater success in obtaining employment. On the other hand, the hypothesis can be entertained that blacks who leave the South in search of better economic opportunities are more willing both to accept the kind of menial work that northern-born blacks have come to reject and to adapt to an economic arrangement which seems to have created permanent economic proletarians out of a substantial percentage of lower-class city residents. If so, this is not unlike the behavior of those migrants from other parts of the world who leave a poorer economy for a more developed economy and who there, in hopes of improving their standard of living, initially tend to accept willingly the kinds of work the indigenous workers have come to reject.

The Decline of Racial Conflict in the Industrial Sector

If the structural changes in the economy have fundamentally altered the job-market situation in central cities, they have also significantly contributed to the changing context of black-white interaction and confrontation. Indeed, nearly all of the major racial flareups in the first half of the twentieth century were directly or indirectly related to labor-market conflicts. The characteristic feature of race relations in the period of industrial race relations was the spillover of economic class conflict between whites to racial conflicts between working-class whites and blacks. And this was as true for the postbellum South in the late nineteenth century as it was for the twentieth-century North during the earlier decades of rapid industrialization and urbanization. However, the labor-market racial flareups of the industrial period have not extended into the modern industrial period. Specifically, whereas blacks posed a distinct threat to white workers as strikebreakers and as a force manipulated by management to undercut white labor in previous years, in the present period the structural relations between blacks and whites in the labor market have significantly reduced racial confrontations over jobs. On the one hand, the shifts in the economy leading to a segmented labor structure have resulted in blacks either being isolated in the low-wage labor market and being concentrated in nonunionized, low-paying, basically undesirable jobs that nobody really wants or readily accepts, or being part of the higher-paying corporate and government industry labor market and thus being protected by powerful unions which effectively control job competition or have rigorous prerequisites that eliminate the poorly trained and educated regardless of race. Moreover, political changes leading, first, to the passage of protective union legislation during the New Deal era and, second, to the equal employment legislation in the early sixties have virtually eliminated the tendency of employers to create a split labor market in which black labor is deemed cheaper than white labor regardless of the work performed, the market that provided for so much of the racial antagonism during the earlier years of the period of industrial race relations.

If there is an imminent potential for racial conflict in the industrial order it would most probably be related to the affirmative action programs that are legally based on Executive Order No. 11246, issued by President Lyndon Johnson in 1965, and have been formally established by the Office of Federal Contract Compliance. However, as I have attempted to show, affirmative action programs are not designed to deal with the problem of the disproportionate concentration of blacks in the low-wage labor market. Their major impact has been in the higher-paying jobs of the expanding service-producing industries in both the corporate and government sectors. The rapid growth of these industries has also contributed to the significant gains that talented and educated blacks have made in white-collar positions. Both qualified whites and blacks have been easily absorbed into these positions, and the continued expansion of corporate and government industries has kept racial friction over higher-paying corporate and government jobs to a minimum.

Thus, in an era of modern industrialism, neither the high-wage corporate and government sectors nor the low-wage sector provides the basis for the kind of interracial competitive conflict that has traditionally plagued the labor market in the United States. And given the structural changes in the American economy and the recent political changes that prohibit racial discrimination, the life chances of individual blacks seem indeed to be based far more on their present economic class position than on their status as black Americans.

To argue that interracial encounters in the economic order have declined is not to suggest that the traditional racial conflicts involved in the struggle for power and privilege have abated. In essence, there has been a gradual shift of racial conflict from the economic to the sociopolitical order. The characteristic feature of the period of modern industrial race relations is that the racial struggle for domination and privilege, with its conflicts and tensions, is heavily concentrated in the sociopolitical order.

The Changing Context of Racial Strife

Just as the structural changes in the economy fundamentally altered the job-market situation in central cities, so too has it contributed to the deepening municipal fiscal crisis and its accompanying racial and social problems, particularly in the industrial centers of the Northeast and Midwest. Few urban analysts would dispute the thesis that the fiscal crisis is inextricably connected with the changing racial and class composition of central cities. I have already shown how industrial expansion provided the opportunity for and gave rise to the twentieth-century migration of rural poor blacks to industrial urban centers. This pattern of migration has continued throughout the 1960s despite the reduction of growth of the goods-producing industries in central cities. The proportion of metropolitan blacks living inside central cities increased from 52 percent in 1960 to 60 percent in 1973 (see table 12), while the proportion of metropolitan whites residing inside central cities decreased from 31 percent to 26 percent. (The white population distribution for the nonmetropolitan areas remained unchanged at 33 percent from 1960 to 1973, while the metropolitan ring population increased from 36 to 41 percent).[54]

It was no coincidence that the white decline in the central city has accompanied the decentralization of American businesses. Residential development in the suburbs has paralleled the expansion of industries outside the central city. Nonetheless, most whites who live in the metropolitan rings continue to work in the central city. The expanding metropolitan expressway system has made it easier for workers to commute from their suburban homes to central-city jobs.

The loss of businesses and higher-income families to the suburbs creates a situation in which central-city tax resources are either declining or are increasing at a decreasing rate. The fiscal problems created by the drop in income and property-tax revenue are further aggravated by the sharp growth in expenditure requirements "triggered by the rising number of 'high cost' citizens."[55] Public welfare statistics clearly and dramatically attest to this fact. Cities such as Chicago and Baltimore account for over 70 percent of the AFDC expenditures in their respective states despite the fact that only 31 percent of Illinois' population is located in Chicago and 27 percent of Maryland's population resides in Baltimore.[56]

In New York City 1.2 million people (or 15.4 percent of the city's total population) were recipients of some form of public assistance in 1975, a figure which represents an increase of 100 percent over the number of New Yorkers on welfare less than a decade ago. In 1965 12 percent of the city's budget was allocated to welfare and 20 percent to elementary and secondary education. By 1970, however, 23 percent of New York City's budget was consumed by welfare and only 18 percent was appropriated for education.[57] In Chicago 9.2 percent (305,468) of the population was receiving public assistance in April of 1970, and that figure had increased to 18.7 percent (605,150) in April of 1975. Moreover, expenditures for urban school systems are accelerating. As Hummel and Nagel have pointed out:

TABLE 12. Population Distribution and Change, Inside and Outside Metropolitan Areas, 1960, 1970, and 1973
(units in thousands)

Area	Black			White		
	1960	1970	1973	1960	1970	1973*
United States	18,872	22,580	23,189	158,832	177,749	179,574
Metropolitan areas	12,741	16,771	17,619	105,829	120,579	120,631
Inside central cities	9,874	13,140	13,868	49,415	49,430	47,206
Outside central cities	2,866	3,630	3,751	56,414	71,148	73,425
Nonmetropolitan areas	6,131	5,810	5,570	53,003	57,170	58,943
% distribution						
United States	100	100	100	100	100	100
Metropolitan Areas	68	74	76	67	68	67
Inside central cities	52	58	60	31	28	26
Outside central cities	15	16	16	36	40	41
Nonmetropolitan areas	32	26	24	33	32	33

Source: U.S. Bureau of the Census, "The Social and Economic Status of the Black Population in the United States, 1973," *Current Population Reports*, Series P-23, no. 48 (Washington, D.C.: Government Printing Office, 1974).
*Five-quarter average centered on April 1973. Quarterly estimates for the months of October 1972 and January, April, July, and October 1973 were used. These figures do not include annexations since 1970.

Most central city school systems find it increasingly difficult to raise sufficient financial resources to meet the dramatically increased social and educational demands placed upon them. The cost of operating public schools in an urban setting increases each year as building and maintenance costs accelerate, staff salaries and wages increase, and expensive special programs are mounted. At the same time, the difficulties faced by all public school districts in their efforts to obtain adequate financial support are aggravated substantially for central city school systems by their need to compete for dollars with a multitude of other social and governmental agencies; by the steady decline in their property tax bases; by their loss of valuable human capital to the suburbs; and by their lack of financial support from state legislatures.[58]

The mounting financial problems of urban schools seem to go hand in hand with their rapidly changing racial composition. In Chicago, the white enrollment in the public schools had dropped from 46.3 percent in 1966 to 24.9 percent in 1976. Other cities have experienced similar changes. In Philadelphia, the black student enrollment has increased to more than 60 percent of the total school population, with most white pupils attending parochial schools. In New York, the black and Puerto Rican public school population increased from 32 percent in 1957 to 63 percent in 1973. The change in the public school population reflects both a change in race and a change in social class as fewer white and middle-class black parents are sending their children to urban public schools. The result has been an exceedingly rapid rise in the proportion of "high cost" disadvantaged students and a corresponding drop in overall educational performance. If the annual reading scores of urban public schools are any indication, children who have the greatest need for education are receiving the poorest training. For example, in the Chicago public schools in 1966-67, only 32 percent of the sixth graders could read at a fourth-grade level. In the low-income neighborhoods of Washington D.C., mean educational achievement "lagged 1.2 years behind the national norm."[59] In the first year of open admissions at the City University of New York, half of the entering freshmen required remedial help in reading and mathematics. "Intensive help had to be given to 10 percent who read at the ninth-grade level or below and to 25 percent whose mathematical achievement was at the eighth-grade level or lower."[60]

Finally, central cities are experiencing increasing difficulty in handling and paying for municipal services. The combination of population density, disproportionate concentration of "high cost" citizens, and the presence of a large commuter force during working hours forces "central cities to spend far more than most suburban neighbors for police and fire protection and sanitation services. The thirty-seven largest central cities had a noneducational (municipal) outlay of $232 per capita in 1965—$100 greater than their suburban counterparts."[61]

Although industrialization encouraged and provided a basis for the continued large migration of poor blacks and other minorities to central cities throughout the 1950s and 1960s, and although the technological and economic changes of the post–World War II period precipitated the movement toward industry decentralization and ultimately the residential development of the suburbs, once these processes were underway they became part of a vicious circle of metropolitan population change and relocation. Specifically, the more revenue lost in income and property taxes from the exodus of a higher-paid labor force and industry, and the more supportive services the increasing numbers of "high cost" citizens demand, the less money there is available for adequate police, education, recreation, and fire protection services; thus the higher costs for deteriorating services simply encourages more industries and people (particularly those economically able to move to the suburbs) to leave.[62]

Accordingly, the flight to the suburbs by the more affluent families has meant that the central cities are increasingly becoming the domain of the poor and the stable working class. According to Tom Kahn, this "reflects not only a racial separation, but an occupational one as well. Most suburbanites are white collar workers in the expanding service-producing sector of the economy. . . . The blue collar workers who live in the suburbs tend to be skilled workers protected by strong unions. Thus, the technological changes in our economy have profoundly affected the composition and layout of the cities."[63]

The changing class and racial composition of central cities has had strong implications for the patterns of racial tension that have accompanied the period of modern industrial race relations. Structural changes in the economy and a series of political changes designed to discourage racial discrimination have eroded the basis for racial conflict and antagonism in the economic sector. Accordingly, the traditional patterns of racial competition for power and privilege are increasingly evidenced in the sociopolitical order. Nonetheless, the key actors on the racial stage remain the same. Just as working-class whites and blacks were the key actors in the major outbreaks of labor-market racial violence during the industrial race relations period, so too are they the central elements in the manifestations of social and political racial antagonism today. Indeed, the racial arena in the central city today increasingly involves a confrontation between working-class whites and poor blacks. This is not to say that there has been any real or apparent increase in the number and severity of racial incidents in recent years, but it is to point out that, unlike in the economic sector, there is a very solid basis for the manifestation of racial violence between lower-income whites and blacks in the sociopolitical order. Both groups have felt the full impact of the urban fiscal crisis. Unlike middle-class whites and blacks, they have been forced by financial exigencies to remain in the central city and suffer the strains of increased crime, higher taxes, poorer services, and inferior public schools. Moreover, unlike the more affluent whites and blacks who choose to remain in the central city, they cannot easily escape the problems of deteriorating public schools by sending their children to private schools. Thus, the racial struggle for power and privilege in the central city is essentially a struggle between the have-nots; it is a struggle over access to and control of decent housing and decent neighborhoods, as exposed by the black-white friction over attempts to integrate the working-class ethnic neighborhood of Marquette Park on Chicago's South Side; it is a struggle over access to and control of local public schools, as demonstrated in the racial violence that followed attempts to bus black children from the Boston ghettoes of Roxbury and Dorchester to the working-class ethnic neighborhoods of South Boston and Charlestown; finally, it is a struggle over political control of the central city, as exhibited in Newark and Cleveland when the race of the mayoralty candidate was the basis for racial antagonism and fear that engulfed the election campaign.

In some cases the conflicts between working-class whites and blacks are expressed in ethnic terms. Thus in a city such as Chicago white working-class ethnics are stressing that their ethnic institutions and unique ways of life are being threatened by black encroachment on their neighborhoods, the increase of black crime, and the growth of black militancy. The emphasis is not simply that blacks pose a threat to whites but that they also pose a threat to, say, the Polish in Gage Park, the Irish in Brighton Park, the Italians in Cicero, or the Serbians, Rumanians, and Croatians in Hegewisch. These communities are a few of the many ethnic communities in the Chicago area threatened by the possibilities of a black invasion, and their response has been to stress not only the interests of whites in general but the interests of their specific ethnic groups as well. The primary issue is whether neighborhood ethnic churches and private ethnic schools can survive if whites leave their communities in great numbers and move either to other parts of the cities or to the suburbs. The threatened survival of ethnic social clubs and the possible loss of ethnic friends are also crucial issues that contribute to the anxiety in these communities.

The fear of black political power was not a crucial issue in Chicago when Mayor Daley was alive and directed his powerful political machine. But it immediately became an issue when the city voted for his successor, and it is reasonable to expect that the racial background of the mayoral candidate will continue to preoccupy Chicagoans in a way not unlike that expressed in other racially tense cities. In the Slovak community on the East Side of Cleveland, for example, residents in the late 1960s verbalized their concerns about the ascendancy of a black politician to the mayoralty and about black encroachment on their neighborhood. One member of the Slovak community put it this way:

> Things were bad before Mayor Stokes, a black, was elected, but since his election, the situation in the neighborhood had quickly become untenable. Stokes is responsible for encouraging blacks to come up from the South and get on Cleveland's welfare and crime rolls. Stokes has allowed

a new permissiveness. The blacks are cocky because one of their own is downtown. It doesn't matter that crime has risen in cities with white mayors. In Cleveland, in the old neighborhood, it is largely Stokes' fault.[64]

These kinds of worries and complaints only serve to heighten the tensions that already exist in racially changing ethnic neighborhoods and to increase the motivation to retreat to the suburbs, leaving the whites who remain the problems of preserving the ethnic institutions in their community. But this is difficult at times. In the late 1960s, the major ethnic church in the Slovak community of Cleveland was on the verge of collapse because the parish was dwindling in numbers; and the Catholic school, which a few decades ago had bulged with 1,100 students, had only 350 with 25 or 30 of those non-Catholics.[65]

Although the research on the recent white response to black encroachment has been limited, there have been a number of recent essays on the reaction of American Jews to black advances. One of the most persuasive is Murray Friedman's perceptive study of Jewish racial attitudes.[66] Friedman points out that whereas Jews as a group tended to identify with the black man's struggle for racial equality prior to the 1960s, sharp division along class lines now characterizes Jewish reaction to blacks. Hostile feelings have emerged among lower-middle-class Jews, who are most "threatened by the black surge forward." Their children attend municipal rather than private or suburban schools, and community or city colleges rather than elite private institutions of higher learning; they live in racially changing neighborhoods, work in marginal-status jobs, and are the most visible and vulnerable targets upon whom blacks in the ghettoes can vent their rage. The Jewish professional class can keep the liberal tradition alive because they do not face the day-to-day challenge from blacks for scarce resources within the inner city, but lower-middle-class Jews are in the immediate path of efforts by blacks to improve their status. The black threat comes from many directions: in the policy of open enrollment, which could reduce the competitive advantage of Jews in entering municipal colleges; in the increasing number of blacks residing in Jewish neighborhoods, which in turn is accelerating the white (Jewish) exodus;

in the emerging black capitalism which is challenging Jewish-owned stores in the ghetto; in the quest for black control of community schools, which could make the positions of Jews as teachers less secure; and in the anti-Semitic rhetoric of black militancy, which increases Jewish insecurity in central cities where Jews as a group are concentrated.

Increasingly, Jewish leaders are talking about the threat that black advancement poses to Jews, and the issues are couched in distinctive ethnic terms. One author reflects on the fears that many Jews have about racial quotas.

> Let me be blunt. If ethnic quotas are to be imposed on American universities and similar quasi-public institutions, it is Jews who will be driven out. They are not 3 percent of the population. This would be a misfortune to them, but a disaster to the nation. And I very much fear that there is a whiff of anti-Semitism in many of these demands.[67]

Although conflict over residential segregation and racially changing neighborhoods was one of the major aspects of racial antagonism throughout the period of industrial race relations, the struggles over access to schools and control of municipalities are fairly recent occurrences brought about by basic changes in the American social structure.[68] In the former case, the political changes designed to prohibit racial discrimination and segregation (changes that emanated from the civil rights era) paved the way for the implementation of desegregation programs. In the latter case, the changing racial composition of the central cities has provided blacks with an opportunity to gain control of urban political systems. Cities such as Washington, D.C., Newark, and Gary already have a majority black population, whereas cities such as Chicago, Cleveland, Philadelphia, Atlanta, St. Louis, and Detroit have approached or are very near to having a third of their population being black. In Chicago, for example, the black population increased from one-seventh of the total population in 1950 to roughly one-third in 1972. This rapid rise in numbers has provided a base for an increasing number of black politicians to run successfully for political office. Indeed by May 1975, there were black mayors in eleven cities with a population size of one hundred thousand or more.[69]

The significance of black political control of the central city is not that it will provide a basis for economic and social mobility in the black community (for as we shall see in the following chapter there is more than sufficient reason to doubt that it will) but that it will heighten the racial antagonism that occasionally surfaces over issues such as school busing and residential segregation. In this connection, Cloward and Piven are probably correct when they argue that: "Black majorities . . . mean the alienation of urban whites. The frequent assertion that in time all whites will simply flee to the suburbs ignores the logistics of finding space for so many people, most of them not wealthy, in the already developed suburban ring. Millions of whites unable or unwilling to leave will remain in the core cities, a fact of key political importance, since they will fiercely resist the exploitation of municipal power for black interests."[70]

Conclusion

As the arguments advanced in this chapter suggest, it would be nearly impossible to comprehend the economic plight of lower-class blacks in the inner city by focusing solely on racial oppression, that is, the overt and explicit effort of whites to keep blacks in a subjugated state. It would also be difficult to explain the rapid economic improvement of the black elite by rigidly postulating the view that the traditional patterns of racial discrimination are still salient in the labor-market practices of American industries. In short, unlike in previous periods of American race relations, economic class is now a more important factor than race in determining job placement for blacks.

Although some writers have argued that the collapse of traditional discriminatory patterns in the labor market has increased job opportunities for all segments of the black population,[71] my analysis suggests that this is not true for the black poor. The patterns of racial oppression in the past created the huge black underclass, as the accumulation of disadvantages were passed on from generation to generation, and the technological and economic revolution of advanced industrial society combined to insure it a permanent status. As a result of the decentralization of American businesses, the movement from goods-producing to service-producing industries, and the clear manifestation of these changes in the expansion of the corporate sector and the government sector, a segmented labor market has developed resulting in vastly different mobility opportunities for different groups in the black population. On the one hand, the relatively poorly trained blacks of the inner city, including the growing number of younger blacks emerging from inferior ghetto schools, find themselves locked in the low-wage sector (operative, laborer, and service-worker jobs) where there is little opportunity for advancement and rates of job turnover are high. On the other hand, the more talented and highly educated blacks are experiencing unprecedented job opportunities in the corporate and government sectors because of the expansion of salaried white-collar positions and the pressures of demonstrated affirmative action.

In addition to the declining significance of race as a factor in determining the position of blacks in the labor market, explanations of racial stratification that associate racial antagonism with labor-market conflicts, such as the economic class theories discussed in Chapter 1, also have little application to the present period of advanced industrial race relations. For as I have attempted to show in this chapter, neither the corporate and government sectors nor the low-wage sector provides the basis for the kind of interracial competition and conflict that characterized the economic order in the previous periods. Racial strife has, in fact, shifted away from the economic sector. The traditional racial struggles for power and privilege are now concentrated in the socio-political order. The main actors are basically the same—blacks and the white working class—but the issues now have more to do with racial control of residential areas, schools, municipal political systems, and recreational areas than with the control of jobs.

6 PROTESTS, POLITICS, AND THE CHANGING BLACK CLASS STRUCTURE

In the preindustrial period of American race relations, very nearly all blacks had not only to confront the day-to-day problems associated with subordination by racial status but also those stemming from subordination by social class. Whether one focuses on the vast majority of enslaved blacks or on the small number of free blacks, their uniformly low economic class position reinforced the racists' views that blacks were not only culturally inferior to whites but biogenetically inferior as well. The question of whether the black experience in this period is better explicated in terms of class or in terms of race has little meaning, for throughout most of the preindustrial period to be black was to be severely deprived of both social and economic resources. Accordingly, if there was meaningful collective variation in the black experience, it pertained to the difference in being a slave as opposed to being a free black, particularly to being a free black in the nineteenth-century antebellum North.

The slave experience was conditioned by the structured relationships with the slave masters—relationships that not only epitomized the extreme differences in racial status and power but also became increasingly paternalistic after the ban on the African slave trade. The very structure of the relationship between master and slave, not to mention the isolation of the latter on rural plantations, effectively prevented the development of a racially militant collective awareness. There were, of course, a few sporadic slave revolts organized by free blacks and slaves who happened to reside in the cities and who were neither under nor influenced by the close, day-to-day plantation supervision. However, the conditions conducive to a successful revolt, or even a large number of attempted revolts, did not exist in the antebellum South. Unlike slaves in Brazil and the Caribbean, bondsmen in the Old South failed to forge a revolutionary tradition or to generate revolts of significant frequency, duration, size, and historical-political magnitude. The structural factors that account for these differences are general conditions that could be meaningfully applied in comparative explanations of slave revolts in other societies. Basically, as Genovese points out, slave insurrections flourished in areas where plantations were very large, where there was a high ratio of slaves to free persons, where the ruling class was divided, where slaves had a chance to acquire military experience, and where the master-slave relations were more business-oriented than paternalistic. None of these factors prevailed in the Old South.[1] Throughout the period of slavery, therefore, blacks were hardly in a position to mount a serious attack against the institution of slavery. They even had to depend on their paternalistic bond with the masters for protection against the abuses of the white lower class which had helplessly, but resentfully, watched slavery erode its economic position in the South.

For free blacks in the antebellum North the situation was somewhat different. They, unlike most southern blacks, were not at the mercy of an overseer or master; they could not be bought and sold; and their families could not be arbitrarily broken up by whites. Although the overwhelming majority of northern free blacks were trapped in menial positions, and although they were frequently victimized by white working-class racial antagonism, a few were able to improve their socioeconomic position. Indeed some northern blacks established successful businesses and accumulated property. By 1860 an increasing number of northern blacks were making use of educational opportunities both in all-black schools and in a small number of integrated schools. Moreover, educated blacks did not passively accept attempts to deprive them of equal rights. The rigid racial order never permitted the types of overt protest characteristic of the late twentieth century, but educated northern blacks did organize and petition, publish newspapers voicing their opposition to racial exploitation, join with white abolitionists to advance civil rights, press political candidates to take a stand against slavery, speak out against political oppression, launch suffrage campaigns, and organize Negro convention movements to devise plans to eliminate racial oppression.[2] Although these protest activities had little real effect, they symbolized the beginning of an organized free black opposition to racial oppression, opposition which varied in intensity, complexity, and style under the changing social conditions of the late nineteenth and twentieth centuries. The protests also underlined the fact that on the eve of the Civil War a small black elite had emerged in the North whose improved class status coincided with increased expressions of dissatisfaction with racial injustice. But it was not until the industrial period of American race relations that one could meaningfully speak of the development of a black middle class and could witness a much clearer manifestation of class-based racial protests.

Industrial Race Relations and the Emergence of a Black Middle Class

The change from a preindustrial to an industrial system of production facilitated and directly contributed to the growth of the urban black community. As Negroes began migrating in significant numbers from the rural South to the nation's burgeoning industrial centers, black enclaves sprang up in various parts of those cities. These Negro neighborhoods reflected both class subordination and racial segregation. Blacks were trapped in the most deteriorated or run-down residential sections not only because of poverty but also because of a stringent pattern of housing discrimination. That the typical black migrant did not escape poverty when he arrived in the city in the first quarter of the twentieth century, although the standard of living in the city was still higher than in the rural South, is seen in the overwhelming concentration of Negroes in the low-status occupations such as domestic and service jobs. Even after black workers entered the goods-producing industries in fairly significant numbers during the World War I period, they rarely advanced beyond the most menial jobs.[3]

Although the vast majority of urban blacks represented the very bottom of the occupational ladder and had few, if any, prospects for occupational advancement, during the first quarter of the twentieth century a class structure within the segregated black community had slowly but definitely taken shape. Essentially, a Negro business and professional class developed hand in hand with the growth of black organizations and institutions to meet the needs of and serve the rapidly expanding black urban population. Before the turn of the century only a handful of blacks (in cities such as Chicago, New York, Washington, D.C.,

Philadelphia, and Baltimore) could be identified as having an economic and status position uniquely and significantly different from the masses. This group constituted, in the words of Allan Spear, "a proud and exclusive elite—men and women who traced their ancestry to ante-bellum free blacks and who frequently had close economic and social ties with the white community."[4] They were firmly committed to the view that America's racial problems could be relieved through integration. In the late nineteenth century their leader was the great abolitionist and integrationist Frederick Douglass, and in the early twentieth century the militant black intellectual W. E. B. Dubois inspired some of them.[5]

However, during the first two decades of the twentieth century, the old black elite was gradually displaced by a new leadership of black businessmen and professionals whose base was in the growing, but segregated, black community and who had little contact or association with the white community. Unlike the old integration-oriented elite (whose contacts in the white community went back not only to the fluid period of race relations from 1870 to 1890 but also to the abolitionist era of the late antebellum period) this new leadership abandoned the dream of integration. As the South was rapidly developing a rigid pattern of Jim Crow segregation, and as race relations in the North deteriorated at the turn of the century, the emerging Negro business and professional class turned inward and espoused the philosophy of self-help and racial solidarity, eloquently articulated on a national level by Booker T. Washington. This small but growing group of black businessmen, ministers, politicians, journalists, and other professionals, excluded from the white community, "worked to create a cohesive and self-sufficient black metropolis. They were the architects of the institutional ghetto."[6] Their hopes for a viable and autonomous black community were quickly dashed, however. Most black businesses were unable to survive because they were undercapitalized and could not obtain credit from white banks. Black social agencies were hardly in a position to confront the problems of the impoverished ghetto because they lacked the financial resources to develop satisfactory facilities and to hire adequate professional staffs. And black politicians, excluded from meaningful participation in the power-

ful urban political machines, could only offer token patronage.
Thus, concludes Spear, "The dream of a black controlled community, growing out of the frustrations of the turn-of-the-century
race relations and nurtured by the population growth of the
World War I era and the 1920's, collapsed with the Depression
—to be revived, in different form of course, in the 1960's."[7]

The Changing Shape of the Black Class Structure

The Depression of the 1930s not only wiped out many of the
small black businesses established during the two previous decades, it also created even greater miseries for the huge black
lower-class population. Indeed, in some of the southern cities as
many as three-fourths of the black population were on relief.[8]
However, the New Deal policies of Franklin D. Roosevelt's administration brought sudden relief to many of the impoverished
black masses and significantly contributed to the growth of occupational differentiation within the black community. Blacks were
employed for the first time as statisticians, lawyers, engineers,
architects, economists, office managers, case aids, librarians, and
interviewers. Lower-level white-collar positions for secretaries,
clerks, and stenographers also became available. Despite the fact
that many of these jobs involved administering governmental
programs for blacks, they represented the first real breakthrough
in a racially segregated labor market.[9]

The role of the state in providing such employment opportunities for blacks is not surprising in view of the increased black
political resources generated by their growing concentration in
northern cities. But more about that in a later section of this
chapter; I have yet to discuss what was one of the most significant contributions to black occupational differentiation during
and following the New Deal era, the improved relationship between black workers and labor unions.

The passage of protective union legislation during the New
Deal era created a favorable climate for collective bargaining and,
as I pointed out in Chapter 4, precipitated a change in organized
labor's relationships with black workers. The importance of the
changing union attitudes and practices toward blacks is perhaps
best conveyed in Bayard Rustin's observation:

Although the new industrial unions were certainly not free of the prejudicial attitudes and policies which permeated the entire society, they made a practice of organizing black and white workers as equals wherever possible. Today this may not seem important, but at the time it was a gesture of revolutionary significance. No other mass institution in American society was so fully open to the participation of blacks; for the first time, Negroes could play an active role in an institution which vigorously sought to change the direction of society.[10]

The increased black participation in labor unions was probably one of the major reasons why the proportion of blacks in semi-skilled and skilled positions increased from 17.2 percent in 1940 to 29.1 percent in 1950 (see table 13). However, to talk about the greater representation of blacks in higher-paying blue-collar jobs is to describe just one of the ways in which blacks experienced occupational change during the decade of the 1940s. If we follow E. Franklin Frazier's lead and identify a black middle class in terms of those who are employed in the white-collar jobs and in the craftsmen and foremen positions,[11] then the proportion of black males in those occupations increased from 9.6 percent in 1940 to 16.4 percent in 1950. Moreover, the proportion of black males in working-class jobs (semiskilled operative positions) in-creased from 12.7 percent in 1940 to 21.3 percent in 1950. Finally, the percentage of black males in essentially lower-class jobs (service workers, farm workers, and unskilled laborers) decreased from 78.1 percent in 1940 to 62.1 percent in 1950.

Thus, on the basis of the occupational distribution of employed males, it appears that roughly only one-third of the black popu-lation could be classified as either working class or middle class at mid-twentieth century.[12] Still, when one considers that the percentage of black males in working- and middle-class jobs in-creased from 22.3 in 1940 to 37.6 in 1950, it is quite clear that a sizable number of blacks experienced occupational mobility dur-ing the decade of the 1940s.[13] Aside from the previously men-tioned factors of more liberal union policies and employment in government industries, black job opportunities also increased during World War II because of the labor shortages and the pas-sage of the Fair Employment Practices Act that outlawed discrimi-

TABLE 13. Percentage of Employed Black Males (Fourteen Years Old and Over) in Major Occupations in 1940, 1950, 1960, and 1970

Occupation	1940	1950	1960	1970
Professional and technical workers	1.8	2.1	4.6	7.0
Proprietors, managers, and officials	1.3	2.2	1.9	3.0
Clerical, sales, etc.	2.0	4.3	6.8	10.2
Craftsmen, foremen, etc.	4.5	7.8	10.7	15.2
Operatives	12.7	21.3	26.6	29.4
Service workers and laborers	37.1	38.1	38.4	32.0
Farm workers	41.0	24.0	12.3	4.4

Source: U.S. Bureau of the Census, *Census of the Population: 1940*, Characteristics of the Nonwhite Population by Race, Table 8; *Census of the Population: 1950*, vol. 4, Special Reports, Nonwhite Population by Race, Table 9; *Census of the Population: 1960*, Subject Reports, Nonwhite Population by Race, Final Report PC(2)-1C, Table 32; *Census of the Population: 1970*, Subject Reports, Final Report PC(2)-1B, Negro Population, Table 7.

nation in the industrial plants holding federal contracts. Although many black workers lost their jobs following the war because defense industries declined and white veterans returned to the civilian labor force, "the conditions remained more favorable for Negro advancement than they had been before the war. Negro servicemen and workers in war industries gained valuable training and experience that enabled them to compete more effectively and their employment in large numbers in the unionized industries during the war left them in a stronger position in the labor market."[14]

The most dramatic changes in black mobility, however, occurred during the decades of the 1950s and 1960s. Whereas 16.4 percent of black males were employed in middle-class occupations in 1950, 24 percent held such jobs in 1960 and 35.3 percent in 1970. Whereas 21.3 percent of black males were in essentially working-class jobs in 1950, 26.6 percent were so employed in 1960 and 29.4 percent in 1970. Finally, whereas 62.1 percent of all black employed males were in basically lower-class jobs in 1950, 50.7 percent held such jobs in 1960 and only 36.4 percent in 1970.

There are several factors involved in this remarkable shift in the black occupational structure. It is clear that the expansion of the economy, that is, the growth of the corporate and government sectors during the 1950s and 1960s, increased white-collar job opportunities for more talented or educated blacks. Moreover, the increased involvement of blacks in unions facilitated their entry into the higher-paying semiskilled and skilled blue-collar jobs. Furthermore, the equal employment legislation, first on the municipal and state levels after World War II and then on the federal level in the 1960s, removed many of the artificial barriers to black employment. Finally, the movement of blacks from the rural South to the industrial centers of the nation sharply decreased the number of blacks working on farms (from 41 percent in 1940 to 4.4 percent in 1970), where so much of black poverty had been concentrated throughout the twentieth century.

Although the changes in the black occupational structure since 1940 quite clearly show a consistent pattern of job upgrading, there are firm indications, as I have emphasized, that in the period of modern industrialization, the chances of continued economic improvement for the black poor are rapidly decreasing. I specifically have in mind the sharp rise in the black unemployment rate for the young and poorly trained ghetto blacks who are entering or have recently entered the labor market and face structural barriers to the higher-paying positions in the central corporate and government industries. Their unemployment rates sharply exceed the rates of other groups in the labor force regardless of swings in the business cycle. Moreover, they have evidenced a steady decline in their labor force participation rates in recent years which means that many of them have given up looking for work altogether. Furthermore, the effects of the advanced industrial, segmented labor market can be gauged by examining the rapid increase in the educational level of workers in the lower-paying occupations (unskilled laborers, service workers, semiskilled operatives) in which blacks are heavily concentrated. This means that persons with only a high school education or less may be increasingly consigned to the most inferior jobs. There is already an indication that the movement of blacks out of lower-paying to higher-paying jobs has slowed considerably in the 1970s. However, given the fact that the nation has been in the throes of a recession during this period, one would hardly expect the rate of black occupational mobility in the first half of the 1970s to keep pace with the rate recorded during the 1960s. As shown in table 14, the rate of black occupational upgrading from 1970 to 1974 is considerably below that of 1964 to 1970. However, although blacks continue to experience a faster rate of job improvement than whites, the movement of blacks into the higher-paying white-collar and skilled crafts positions is occurring at a faster rate (5.9 percent) than the movement of blacks out of low-paying service worker and laborer jobs (2.3 percent); the percentage difference between the growth of middle-class jobs and the decline of lower-class jobs was only 1.6 between 1964 and 1970, with black white-collar and skilled craft workers increasing by 10.3 percent and service workers and unskilled laborers decreasing by 8.9 percent.

There are other indications that the poor blacks' economic situation is deteriorating. After a steady decrease in the percentage of black families below the low-income level (from 48.1 percent in 1959 to 29.4 percent in 1968) the proportion of poor

TABLE 14. Percentage of Employed Persons Sixteen Years and Over, by Occupation Group and Color for 1964, 1970, and 1974

Occupation	1964		1970		1974	
	White	Black and other races	White	Black and other races	White	Black and other races
Professional and technical	13.0	6.8	14.8	9.1	14.8	10.4
Managers and administrators	11.7	2.6	11.4	3.5	11.2	4.1
Sales workers	6.6	1.7	6.7	2.1	6.8	2.3
Clerical workers	16.3	7.7	18.0	13.2	17.8	15.2
Craft and similar workers	13.7	7.1	13.5	8.2	13.8	9.4
Operatives	18.4	20.5	17.0	23.7	15.5	21.9
Service workers and laborers	14.6	45.2	14.8	36.3	16.4	34.0
Farm workers	5.8	8.4	4.0	3.4	3.6	2.7

Source: U.S. Department of Labor, *Manpower Report of the President* (Washington, D.C.: Government Printing Office, 1975).

black families has remained around 28 percent from 1969 (27.9 percent) to 1974 (27.8 percent).[15] Moreover, female heads of poor black households increased from 56 percent in 1970 to 67 percent in 1974, and 75 percent of poor black female-headed families received some or all of their income from public assistance in 1973.[16]

Reflecting the increase in black female-headed families, the percentage of black children living with both parents decreased markedly from 64 in 1970 to 56 in 1974.[17] However, as shown in Table 15, for both black and white families, the percentage of children living with both parents is strongly associated with income level. This relationship is even stronger among black families than among white families. For example, in 1974, only 18 percent of the children in black families with incomes of less than $4,000 lived with both parents, while 90 percent of the children in families with incomes of $15,000 or more lived with both parents. The comparable figures for white families are 39 percent and 97 percent. Accordingly, to suggest categorically that the problem of female-headed households is characteristic of black families is to overlook the powerful influence of economic class background. The increase in female-headed households among poor blacks is a consequence of the fact that the poorly trained and educated black males have increasingly restricted opportunities for higher-paying jobs and thus find it increasingly difficult to satisfy the expectations of being a male breadwinner.[18] Moreover, as Carol Stack, in her sensitive analysis of poor black families, has pointed out, "caretaker agencies such as public welfare are insensitive to individual attempts for social mobility. A woman may be immediately cut off the welfare roles when a husband returns from prison, the army, or if she gets married. Thus, the society's welfare system collaborates in weakening the position of the black male."[19]

Not only is there a stronger relationship between female-headed households and social class among black families than among white families, but there is also a more unequal income distribution among black families than among white families. In 1970, the economist Andrew Brimmer pointed out that the lowest two-fifths of nonwhite families in 1969 contributed only 15.3 percent to the total nonwhite income, whereas the lowest two-fifths

TABLE 15. Own Children under Eighteen Years by Presence of Parents and Family Income, 1974 (Income, in current dollars, refers to income received during 1973)

Family Income	Own Black Children			Own White Children		
	Total (thousands)	% living with		Total (thousands)	% living with	
		Both	One		Both	One
Under $4,000	2,031	18	82	3,382	39	61
$4,000–$5,999	1,472	35	65	3,413	66	34
$6,000–$7,999	1,273	53	47	4,260	77	23
$8,000–$9,999	914	78	22	5,321	88	12
$10,000 and over	2,910	88	12	38,949	96	4
$10,000–$14,999	1,600	86	14	16,179	94	6
$15,000 and over	1,310	90	10	22,770	97	3

Source: U.S. Bureau of the Census, "The Social and Economic Status of the Black Population in The United States, 1974," *Current Population Reports*, Series P-23 no. 54, (Washington, D.C.: Government Printing Office, 1975).
Note: Universe is own unmarried children under eighteen years old living in families where at least one parent is present.

of white families provided 18.7 percent of the total white in-come; conversely, the upper two-fifths among white families con-tributed 63.7 percent of the total white income, whereas the upper two-fifths among nonwhite families provided 68.2 percent of the total nonwhite income. After reviewing income data in the 1960s, Brimmer concludes that, unlike among whites, the income gap among blacks seems to be widening.[20]

There has been an uneven development of economic resources in the black community that is not reflected in the changes in the black occupational distribution over the last several decades. For unlike more affluent blacks, the black poor have been plagued by higher unemployment rates, lower labor-force participation rates, higher welfare rates, and, more recently, a slower move-ment out of poverty. For all these reasons, one has to give con-siderable credence to Brimmer's warning that there is a deep-ening economic schism in the black community,[21] a schism that has become especially evident during the economic recession period of the 1970s. And since the structural barriers to occupa-tional advancement were evident even during the high business-activity years in the late 1960s, even an economic recovery is not likely to reverse the pattern of unemployment, underemploy-ment, poverty, welfare, and female-headed households. In short, there are clear indications that the economic gap between the black underclass (close to a third of the black population)[22] and the higher-income blacks will very likely widen and solidify.

Ideology, Racial Protest, and the Changing Black Class Structure

If history tells us anything about the black experience it is that the different expressions of black protest tend often to be a by-product of economic class position. Although it is difficult at this point to determine the effect of the present economic gap be-tween the black poor and the more affluent blacks on racial ideology and protest, there are some concrete observations that can be made about social class and the recent black protest movements.

One major effect of the changes in the black occupational structure after 1940 was the revival of the integrationist ideology and concern for civil rights that had preoccupied black leaders prior to the pessimistic period of self-help and racial solidarity at the turn of the century. "This generation of clerks, teachers, and postmen," states historian John Bracey, "had achieved a sufficient degree of economic security to be able to direct their attention to issues such as integrated education, open housing and free access to public accommodations, and they had the financial resources to support organizations like the N.A.A.C.P., the Urban League, and the numerous local human relations committees that acted in their behalf."[23]

The civil rights organizations effectively pressed for the passage of enforceable bills against discrimination in northern states. In 1945 the New York state legislature enacted the Ives-Quinn Bill, which established the State Commission Against Discrimination, and New Jersey created a division against racial discrimination in the Department of Education. In 1946 Massachusetts established a Fair Employment Practices Commission, and by 1965 twenty-five states and numerous municipalities had established similar commissions.[24] It was no coincidence that in many of the states in which civil rights laws were passed blacks had achieved significant political strength as a result of their increasing concentration in key industrial centers. Indeed, organizations such as the NAACP stressed the importance of the black vote when they pressed politicians to support civil rights legislation.

The mobilization of black political resources was not confined to the state and local levels, however. For example, the NAACP stepped up its litigation efforts and in 1954 won a favorable ruling in *Brown v. Board of Education* that overturned the "separate but equal" doctrine established in the *Plessy v. Ferguson* decision of 1896, and the proliferation of civil rights protests helped to generate the 1964 civil rights bill and the 1965 voting rights bill.

These federal, state, and municipal civil rights acts were mainly due to the efforts of the black professional groups (ministers, lawyers, teachers), students, and, particularly in the 1960s, sympathetic white liberals. Lower-income blacks had little involvement in civil rights politics up to the mid-1960s. As indicated in Chapter 4, blacks throughout the industrial period of race relations were denied access to the structural avenues for political participation (the urban political machines) and could only exert their influence through the extra-institutional civil rights movement. The movement had, as Martin Kilson has noted, a class and status bias and it tended to operate with little direct relationship to the black ghetto.[25] It was not until the latter half of the 1960s that the ghetto blacks significantly determined the nature and direction of black politics.

The prelude to the active involvement of ghetto blacks in politics was the nonviolent resistance campaigns of the early 1960s. The distinctive feature of these protests, which took the form of sit-ins, freedom rides, and the like, was that they were led and organized by educated blacks, many of whom were college students. These black activists recognized and clearly articulated the view that because of the increasing black political resources, the pressures of nonviolent protests, and the United States' concern for world-wide opinion of her racial crisis, the government was likely to react to a disciplined nonviolent movement for civil rights with the enactment of antidiscrimination laws. They were correct. The passage of the 1964 civil rights bill (which outlawed, among other things, discrimination in public facilities, public accommodations, and employment) clearly demonstrated the success of the nonviolent protests against racial injustice. This legislation and the voting rights bill of 1965 (which was intended to enforce the Fifteenth Amendment to the Constitution) and the civil rights bill of 1968 (which banned discrimination in the rental or sale of homes, except for single-family houses sold by the owner himself) were particularly relevant to the growing black middle class that was not concerned about the day-to-day problems of economic survival. However, this legislation did not sufficiently address the unique problems of de facto segregation and social class subordination confronting ghetto blacks.

Nonetheless, although the racial issues that were defined and articulated by black activists in the early 1960s reflected the orientations and specific needs of the growing black middle class, the civil rights protests did in fact heighten lower-class black awareness of racial inequality. With electronic media penetrating the ghetto and covering all aspects of the civil rights protest movement, including the often violent resistance to racial change by white southerners, ghetto blacks, like blacks in all walks of life throughout the country, developed an impatience with the pace of racial change.[26] Indeed it was the violent southern white resistance to racial protest that probably had the greatest effect in increasing militancy among various segments of the black population in the middle 1960s. It is not surprising that white southerners, particularly the white lower class, provided such firm resistance to the civil rights movement. Blacks made up nearly 40 percent of the southern population in the years following the Civil War; they were central to the economy as cheap laborers; and they were highly visible in virtually every region of the South. They proved to be particularly worrisome for the white lower-class masses, who were also victimized by poverty and illiteracy.[27] It was this concern that motivated the most threatened of white southerners to attempt to eliminate black competition after the collapse of Reconstruction. And they did it well. The Jim Crow system of segregation was virtually unchallenged until the 1950s. As long as blacks "kept their place," white southerners exhibited little outward hostility. But the 1954 Supreme Court decision and the nonviolent demonstrations in the South threatened the "southern way of life," and the most violent resistance to racial change came from lower-class whites who felt that they had the most to lose by black encroachment. As white resistance to civil rights protests increased in the South, black bitterness, disgust, and disappointment over the pace of racial change also increased. In the urban ghetto these feelings were dramatically expressed in a series of violent revolts that erupted across the nation in the late 1960s.

It would be difficult to explain the ghetto revolts of the 1960s without relating them to the black disillusionment and anger following the violent white resistance to racial change. However, as I have argued elsewhere, this sense of anger and frustration was combined with specific grievances over unemployment, underemployment, inferior education, inadequate housing, and police brutality.[28] Although these conditions have characterized ghetto living throughout the twentieth century, they seemed all the more intolerable to poor urban blacks in the face of their greater sensitivity to and awareness of racial oppression. As black leaders began to articulate these problems and focus on ways to solve them, the issue of civil rights, which had preoccupied middle-class blacks, was overshadowed by concerns that related more specifically to class subordination in the urban ghetto. Thus, in the late 1960s, some black leaders dramatically proclaimed that, for the black underclass, the question of human rights is far more fundamental than the question of civil rights. The late Martin Luther King was one of the first civil rights leaders to recognize the unique problems of poor Negroes, when he raised the pointed question, "What good is it to be allowed to eat in a restaurant if you can't afford a hamburger?"

If nothing else, the ghetto revolts of the late 1960s helped to shift the philosophy of the black protest movement. People who had been active in the civil rights movement began to focus on ways to erase the cycle of poverty, unemployment, and poor education. At the same time the federal government's "War on Poverty," initiated partly in response to the riots, provided one major mechanism for the institutionalization of ghetto-based politics. Over two thousand community action programs were formed around the country. Although the result was not intended by federal authorities, these programs were often transformed from community service agencies into local political structures staffed and directed by lower-class militants. Across the country the lower-class leaders used these agencies in efforts to politicize the heretofore politically inactive ghetto blacks (welfare mothers, gangs, unskilled and semiskilled workers, school dropouts).[29]

Black professional politicians were also caught up in this new mobilization of political power. With the increased politicization of the black lower class, black middle-class politicians found it necessary to articulate in a more forceful manner the particular needs and problems of their constituencies. This resulted in a shift from a middle-class-based politics to a lower-class-based politics, a shift from a politics whose issues emerged from the concerns of professional civil rights organizations and which focused primarily on problems of race discrimination, to a politics whose issues were defined in response to the urban unrest of the 1960s and which focused on problems of de facto segregation, class subordination, welfare state measures, and human survival in the ghetto.[30]

The changing emphasis in black politics was also accompanied by the revival of the philosophy of racial solidarity growing out of the Black Power movement. Although the Black Power movement, like similar racial solidarity movements of the past, was a response to the frustrations encountered in the scope, pace, and quality of racial change (particularly the resistance to race protest in the South which led leaders such as Stokely Carmichael and H. Rap Brown to question the nonviolent resistance philosophy of moral persuasion and interracialism), its basic ideology guided many of the efforts to politically mobilize the black community. Thus for some black militants the development of black political power not only pertains to control of the basic institutions in the black community but also to political control of the central city. The significance and meaning of such political power in the age of modern industrialization is a subject to which I now turn.

Black Political Control of the Declining Central City

The dilemma for urban blacks is that they are gaining political influence in large urban areas (in 1975 blacks were mayors of eleven large metropolitan cities with populations of one hundred thousand or more)[31] at the very time when the political power and influence of the cities are on the wane. The growth of corporate manufacturing, of retail and wholesale trade on the metropolitan periphery; the steady migration of impoverished minorities to the central city; the continuous exodus of the more affluent families to the suburbs; and, consequently, the relative decline of the central-city tax base have made urban politicians increasingly dependent on state and federal sources of funding in order to maintain properly the services that are vital for community health and stability.[32] Whereas state and federal funds contributed about 25 percent to major-city revenues a decade ago, their contribution today amounts to about 50 percent. Thus America's metropolises are increasingly controlled by politicians whose constituencies do not necessarily live in those cities.[33]

It is this *politics of dependency* that changes the meaning and reduces the significance of the greater black participation in urban political processes. And the militant cry of "black control of the central city" has a hollow ring when one confronts the hard reality of the deepening urban fiscal crisis that has developed in the wake of industry dispersion and urban population shifts. When we consider facts such as those which show that the aggregate income of families and unrelated individuals *entering* the central city between 1970 and 1973 was only 26 billion dollars, whereas the income of those *leaving* was roughly 55 billion dollars,[34] it becomes clear that the internal resources needed by urban politicians to deal with the problems of the city continue to decrease. To suggest therefore that the solution to the problems of the black poor is dependent on blacks gaining political control of the central city is to ignore the fact that the fundamental bases of the urban crisis are not amenable to urban political solutions. Perhaps Katznelson best sums the matter up when he argues that:

> Neither demographic patterns nor poverty rates are caused in the cities, nor are they susceptible to much manipulation at that level. Urban authorities and citizens can hardly control the characteristics of the national economy, including its rate of growth and the nature of the demand for labor; nor can they control characteristics of the industry in which an individual is employed such as profit rates, technology, unionization and the industry's relationship to government, or individual characteristics like age, ethnicity and class, which affect employability. Migration patterns, too, depend heavily on "push" factors over which the receiving cities have virtually no control.[35]

Despite the fact that racial friction is more a symptom than a cause of the declining central city, the urban crisis is often depicted or described as a racial crisis, and the proposed solutions advanced in different quarters (for example, black political control of the city, school desegregation, and residential integration) are often directed at altering the patterns of racial interaction or dominance. Nonetheless, the way that urban families are affected by or are responding to the problems of urban living are more a function of their economic class position than of their racial status. Thus, the declining growth of the manufacturing, wholesale, and retail industries in the central city creates problems for many lower-income whites and blacks but has had little impact on the white and black middle class, whose members have access to the higher-paying white-collar jobs in the expanding service-producing industries in the central city. Moreover, the deterioration of the urban public schools is not as much a problem for middle-income whites and blacks because they have the live option of private-school education; and although middle-class blacks have greater difficulty than middle-class whites in finding housing, their economic resources provide them with more opportunities to find desirable housing and neighborhoods within either the central city or the suburbs than both lower-income blacks and lower-income whites.[36] Since the greater options open to black and white middle-income groups make them less susceptible to racial confrontation in the central city, it is the lower-income groups which are the direct recipients of racial antagonism emanating from the continuing struggle for moderately priced housing in the remaining stable neighborhoods, for access to the more adequate public schools, for the use of inexpensive recreational areas, and for political control of the central city.

Conclusion

In the first part of this chapter I tried to show how the growth of a black middle-class population accompanied the shift from a preindustrial to an industrial system of production. In the early twentieth century a Negro professional and business class developed to meet the needs of and serve the rapidly expanding black population. Disillusioned by the racial setbacks in both the North and the South at the turn of the century, this group of professionals and businessmen trumpeted the ideology of racial solidarity and pressed for the creation of a viable, self-sufficient black metropolis, only to see their hopes shattered by the ravages of the Depression. However, the New Deal marked the beginning of a progressive pattern of occupational upgrading of the black population. Specifically, the more liberal racial policies of labor unions, the increasing black employment in government, the expansion of black job opportunities in the private sector during and following World War II (as a result of the Fair Employment Practices Act and the labor shortage during the war and the expansion of the economy following the war) sharply increased the ranks of working-class and middle-class blacks by mid-twentieth century. Continued expansion of the economy during the 1950s and 1960s, the increased black union membership, the municipal, state, and federal equal employment legislation, and the continued migration of blacks from the rural South to the industrial cities of the nation resulted in an even greater increase of blacks from lower-paying to higher-paying jobs. By 1970 the black occupational structure, which only three decades earlier reflected an overwhelming concentration of Negroes in the low-paying service worker, unskilled laborer, and farm worker jobs, revealed a substantial majority of black workers in white-collar positions and higher-paying blue-collar positions.

I have been careful to point out, however, that the impressive occupational gains made by blacks during these three decades have been partly offset by the effects of basic structural changes in our modern industrial economy, changes that are having differential impact on the different income groups in the black community. Unlike more affluent blacks, many of whom continued to experience improved economic opportunity even during the recession period of the 1970s, the black underclass has evidenced higher unemployment rates, lower labor-force participation rates, higher welfare rates, and, more recently, a sharply declining movement out of poverty. The net effect has been a deepening economic schism in the black community that could very easily widen and solidify.

Considering the changes in the black occupational structure from the industrial to the modern industrial period of American race relations, I have tried to show the connection between social class and the recent black protest movement. I pointed out that, as the ranks of the black middle class swelled, as more and more blacks achieved economic security, attention was directed to issues such as integration and civil rights politics, issues that had preoccupied black leaders prior to the pessimistic period of racial solidarity at the turn of the century. Thus, it was the more educated blacks who led the civil rights campaigns in the late 1950s and early 1960s, and effectively used civil rights politics in achieving the passage of various municipal, state, and federal civil rights laws. However, I argued that although the civil rights movement reflected the needs and interests of the black middle class, it did not sufficiently address the unique problems of class subordination and de facto segregation in the black ghetto. Indeed ghetto blacks had little direct involvement in the civil rights protests. However, the very activity of the civil rights activists had the effect of increasing lower-class black awareness of and impatience with racial oppression. And these feelings exploded in a proliferation of ghetto riots in the late 1960s. If nothing else, the revolts led black leaders to redefine the problems of poor blacks and paved the way for a shift from a middle-class-based black politics to a lower-class-based black politics. This shift in black politics was also accompanied by the new strategies of black political power that grew out of the Black Power movement, including the avowed goal, in some quarters, of gaining black political control of the central city.

However, as I emphasized, blacks are gaining urban political influence at the very time when the city, as a base of political power, is on the decline. And, the problems created by population shifts, industry dispersion, and other basic economic changes cannot be sufficiently addressed by urban political solutions.

7

THE DECLINING SIGNIFICANCE OF RACE

This study has revealed that although racial oppression, when viewed from the broad perspective of historical change in American society, was a salient and important feature during the pre-industrial and the industrial periods of race relations in the United States, the problems of subordination for certain segments of the black population and the experiences of social advancement for others are more directly associated with economic class in the modern industrial period. In arriving at this conclusion, I have been careful to recognize the manner in which economic and political changes have gradually shaped a black class structure, making it increasingly difficult to speak of a single or uniform black experience. Although a small elite population of free, propertied blacks did in fact exist during the antebellum period, the interaction between race and economic class only assumed real importance for blacks in the late part of the industrial era of race relations; the significance of this relationship has grown as the nation has entered the modern industrial period. In this chapter I should like, by way of summary and conclusion, to outline some of the basic theoretical and substantive arguments I have advanced regarding racial change in America and to redefine some of the problems that are generally perceived as racial in nature.

Each of the major periods of American race relations has been shaped in different measure both by the systems of production and by the laws and policies of the state. However, the relationships between the economy and the state have varied in each period and therefore the roles of both institutions in shaping race relations have differed over time.

In the preindustrial period the slave-based plantation economy of the South allowed a relatively small, elite group of planters to develop enormous regional power. The hegemony of the southern ruling elite was based on a system of production that required little horizontal or vertical mobility and therefore could be managed very efficiently with a simple division of labor that virtually excluded free white labor. As long as free white workers were not central to the process of reproducing the labor supply in the southern plantation economy, slavery as a mode of production facilitated the slaveholder's concentration and consolidation of economic power. And the slaveholders successfully transferred their control of the economic system to the political and legal systems in order to protect their class interest in slavery. In effect, the polity in the South regulated and reinforced the system of racial caste oppression depriving both blacks and nonslaveholding whites of any meaningful influence in the way that slavery was used in the economic life of the South. In short, the economy provided the basis for the development of the system of slavery and the polity reinforced and perpetuated that system. Furthermore, the economy enabled the slaveholders to develop a regional center of power and the polity was used to legitimate that power. Since nonslaveholding whites were virtually powerless both economically and politically, they had very little effect on the developing patterns of race relations. The meaningful forms of black-white contact were between slaves and slaveholders, and southern race relations consequently assumed a paternalistic quality involving the elaboration and specification of duties, norms, rights, and obligations as they pertained to the use of slave labor and the system of indefinite servitude.

In short, the pattern of race relations in the antebellum South was shaped first and foremost by the system of production. The very nature of the social relations of production meant that the exclusive control of the planters would be derived from their position in the production process, which ultimately led to the creation of a juridical system that reflected and protected their class interests, including their investment in slavery.

However, in the nineteenth-century antebellum North the form of racial oppression was anything but paternalistic. Here a more industrial system of production enabled white workers to become more organized and physically concentrated than their southern counterparts. Following the abolition of slavery in the North, they used their superior resources to generate legal and informal practices of segregation that effectively prevented blacks from becoming serious economic competitors. As the South gradually moved from a plantation to an industrial economy in the last quarter of the nineteenth century, landless whites were finally

able to effect changes in the racial stratification system. Their
efforts to eliminate black competition helped to produce an
elaborate system of Jim Crow segregation. Poor whites were
aided not only by their number but also by the development of
political resources which accompanied their greater involvement
in the South's economy.

Once again, however, the system of production was the major
basis for this change in race relations, and once again the political system was used to reinforce patterns of race emanating from
structural shifts in the economy. If the racial laws in the antebellum South protected the class interests of the planters and reflected their overwhelming power, the Jim Crow segregation laws
of the late nineteenth century reflected the rising power of white
laborers; and if the political power of the planters was grounded
in the system of production in a plantation economy, the emerging political power of the workers grew out of the new division
of labor that accompanied industrialization.

Except for the brief period of fluid race relations in the North
between 1870 and 1890 and in the South during the Reconstruction era, racial oppression is the single best term to characterize
the black experience prior to the twentieth century. In the antebellum South both slaves and free blacks occupied what could be
best described as a caste position in the sense that realistic
chances for occupational mobility simply did not exist. In the
antebellum North a few free blacks were able to acquire some
property and improve their socioeconomic position, and a few
were even able to make use of educational opportunities. However, the overwhelming majority of free northern Negroes were
trapped in menial positions and were victimized by lower-class
white antagonism, including the racial hostilities of European
immigrant ethnics, who successfully curbed black economic competition. In the postbellum South, the system of Jim Crow segregation wiped out the small gains blacks had achieved during
Reconstruction, and blacks were rapidly pushed out of the more
skilled jobs they had held since slavery. Accordingly, there was
very little black occupational differentiation in the South at the
turn of the century.

Just as the shift from a plantation economy to an industrializing economy transformed the class and race relations in the post-

bellum South, so too did industrialization in the North change the context for race-class interaction and confrontation there. On the one hand, the conflicts associated with the increased black-white contacts in the early twentieth-century North resembled the forms of antagonism that soured the relations between the races in the postbellum South. Racial conflicts between blacks and whites in both situations were closely tied to class conflicts among whites. On the other hand, there were some fundamental differences. The collapse of the paternalistic bond between blacks and the southern business elite cleared the path for the almost total subjugation of blacks in the South and resulted in what amounted to a united white racial movement that solidified the system of Jim Crow segregation. However, a united white movement against blacks never really developed in the North. In the first quarter of the twentieth century, management attempted to undercut white labor by using blacks as strikebreakers and, in some situations, as permanent replacements for white workers who periodically demanded higher wages and more fringe benefits. Indeed the determination of industrialists to ignore racial norms of exclusion and to hire black workers was one of the main reasons why the industry-wide unions reversed their racial policies and actively recruited black workers during the New Deal era. Prior to this period the overwhelming majority of unskilled and semiskilled blacks were nonunionized and were available as lower-paid labor or as strikebreakers. The more management used blacks to undercut white labor, the greater were the racial antagonisms between white labor and black labor. Moreover, racial tension in the industrial sector often reinforced and sometimes produced racial tension in the social order. The growth of the black urban population created a housing shortage during the early twentieth century which frequently produced black "invasions" or ghetto "spillovers" into adjacent poor white neighborhoods. The racial tensions emanating from labor strife seemed to heighten the added pressures of racial competition for housing, neighborhoods, and recreational areas. Indeed, it was this combination of racial friction in both the economic sector and the social order that produced the bloody riots in East St. Louis, in 1917, and in Chicago and several other cities, in 1919.

In addition to the fact that a united white movement against blacks never really developed in the North during the industrial period, it was also the case that the state's role in shaping race relations was much more autonomous, much less directly related to developments in the economic sector. Thus, in the brief period of fluid race relations in the North from 1870 to 1890, civil rights laws were passed barring discrimination in public places and in public institutions. This legislation did not have any real significance to the white masses at that time because, unlike in the pre–Civil War period in the North, and unlike in the post–Civil War period in the South, white workers did not perceive blacks as major economic competitors. Blacks constituted only a small percentage of the total population in Northern cities; they had not yet been used in any significant numbers as cheap labor in industry or as strikebreakers, and their earlier antebellum competitors for low-status jobs (the Irish and German immigrants) had improved their economic status in the trades and municipal employment.

For all these reasons liberal whites and black professionals, urged on by the spirit of racial reform that had developed during the Civil War and Reconstruction, could pursue civil rights programs without firm resistance; for all these reasons racial developments on the political front were not directly related to the economic motivations and interests of workers and management. In the early twentieth century the independent effect of the political system was displayed in an entirely different way. The process of industrialization had significantly altered the pattern of racial interaction, giving rise to various manifestations of racial antagonism. Although discrimination and lack of training prevented blacks from seeking higher-paying jobs, they did compete with lower-class whites for unskilled and semiskilled factory jobs and they were used by management to undercut the white workers' union movement. Despite the growing importance of race in the dynamics of the labor market, the political system did not intervene either to mediate the racial conflicts or to reinforce the pattern of labor-market racial interaction generated by the system of production. This was the case despite the salience of a racist ideology system that justified and prescribed unequal treatment for Afro-Americans. (As was pointed out in Chapter 1, industrialists will more likely challenge societal racial norms in situations where adherence to them results in economic losses.) If nothing else, the absence of political influence on the labor market probably reflected the power struggles between management and workers. Thus, legislation to protect the rights of black workers to compete openly for jobs would have conflicted with the interests of white workers, whereas legislation to deny black participation in any kind of industrial work would have conflicted with the interests of management. To repeat, unlike in the South, a united white movement resulting in the almost total segregation of the work force never really developed in the North.

But the state's lack of influence in the industrial sector of private industries did not mean that it had no significant impact on racial stratification in the early twentieth-century North. The urban political machines, controlled in large measure by working-class ethnics who were often in direct competition with blacks in the private industrial sector, systematically gerrymandered black neighborhoods and excluded the urban black masses from meaningful political participation throughout the early twentieth century. Control by the white ethnics of the various urban political machines was so complete that blacks were never really in a position to compete for the more important municipal political rewards such as patronage jobs or government contracts and services. Thus, the lack of racial competition for municipal political rewards did not provide the basis for racial tension and conflict in the urban political system. And, to repeat, this political racial oppression had no direct connection with or influence on race relations in the private industrial sector.

In sum, whether one focuses on the way race relations was structured by the system of production or the polity or both, racial oppression (ranging from the exploitation of black labor by the business class to the elimination of black competition for economic, social, and political resources by the white masses) was a characteristic and important phenomenon in both the preindustrial and industrial periods of American race relations.

Nonetheless, and despite the prevalence of various forms of racial oppression, the change from a preindustrial to an industrial system of production did enable blacks to increase their political and economic resources. The proliferation of jobs created by industrial expansion helped generate and sustain the continuous mass migration of blacks from the rural South to the cities of the North and West. As the black urban population grew and became more segregated, institutions and organizations in the black community also developed, together with a business and professional class affiliated with these institutions. Still it was not until after World War II (the modern industrial period), that the black class structure started to take on some of the characteristics of the white class structure.

It is also the case that class has become more important than race in determining black life-chances in the modern industrial period. Moreover, the center of racial conflict has shifted from the industrial sector to the sociopolitical order. Although these changes can be related to the more fundamental changes in the system of production and in the laws and policies of the state, the relations between the economy and the polity in the modern industrial period have differed from those in previous periods. In the preindustrial and industrial periods the basis of structured racial inequality was primarily economic, and in most situations the state was merely an instrument to reinforce patterns of race relations that grew directly out of the social relations of production.[1] Except for the brief period of fluid race relations in the North from 1870 to 1890, the state was a major instrument of racial oppression. State intervention in the modern industrial period has been designed to promote racial equality, and the relationship between the polity and the economy has been much more reciprocal, so much so that it is difficult to determine which one has been more important in shaping race relations since World War II. It was the expansion of the economy that facilitated black movement from the rural areas to the industrial centers and that created job opportunities leading to greater occupational differentiation in the black community (in the sense that an increasing percentage of blacks moved into white-collar positions and semiskilled and skilled blue-collar positions); and it was the intervention of the state (responding to the pressures of increased black political resources and to the racial protest movement) that removed many artificial discrimination barriers by municipal, state, and federal civil rights legislation, and that contributed to the more liberal racial policies of the nation's labor unions by protective union legislation. And these combined political and economic changes created a pattern of black occupational upgrading that resulted, for example, in a substantial drop in the percentage of black males in the low-paying service, unskilled laborer, and farm jobs (from close to 80 percent in 1940 to only 36 percent in 1970).

However, despite the greater occupational differentiation within the black community, there are now signs that the effect of some aspects of structural economic change has been the closer association between black occupational mobility and class affiliation. Access to the means of production is increasingly based on educational criteria (a situation which distinguishes the modern industrial from the earlier industrial system of production) and thus threatens to solidify the position of the black underclass. In other words, a consequence of the rapid growth of the corporate and government sectors has been the gradual creation of a segmented labor market that currently provides vastly different mobility opportunities for different segments of the black population. On the one hand, poorly trained and educationally limited blacks of the inner city, including that growing number of black teenagers and young adults, see their job prospects increasingly restricted to the low-wage sector, their unemployment rates soaring to record levels (which remain high despite swings in the business cycle), their labor-force participation rates declining, their movement out of poverty slowing, and their welfare roles increasing. On the other hand, talented and educated blacks are experiencing unprecedented job opportunities in the growing government and corporate sectors, opportunities that are at least comparable to those of whites with equivalent qualifications. The improved job situation for the more privileged blacks in the corporate and government sectors is related both to the expansion of salaried white-collar positions and to the pressures of state affirmative action programs.

In view of these developments, it would be difficult to argue that the plight of the black underclass is solely a consequence of racial oppression, that is, the explicit and overt efforts of whites to keep blacks subjugated, in the same way that it would be difficult to explain the rapid economic improvement of the more privileged blacks by arguing that the traditional forms of racial segregation and discrimination still characterize the labor market in American industries. The recent mobility patterns of blacks lend strong support to the view that economic class is clearly more important than race in predetermining job placement and occupational mobility. In the economic realm, then, the black experience has moved historically from economic racial oppression experienced by virtually all blacks to economic subordination for the black underclass. And as we begin the last quarter of the twentieth century, a deepening economic schism seems to be developing in the black community, with the black poor falling further and further behind middle- and upper-income blacks.

If race is declining in significance in the economic sector, explanations of racial antagonism based on labor-market conflicts, such as those advanced by economic class theories of race, also have less significance in the period of modern industrial race relations. Neither the low-wage sector nor the corporate and government sectors provide the basis for the kind of interracial job competition and conflict that plagued the economic order in previous periods. With the absorption of blacks into industry-wide labor unions, the protective union legislation, and the equal employment legislation, it is no longer possible for management to undercut white labor by using black workers. The traditional racial struggles for power and privilege have shifted away from the economic sector and are now concentrated in the sociopolitical order. Although poor blacks and poor whites are still the main actors in the present manifestations of racial strife, the immediate source of the tension has more to do with racial competition for public schools, municipal political systems, and residential areas than with the competition for jobs.

To say that race is declining in significance, therefore, is not only to argue that the life chances of blacks have less to do with race than with economic class affiliation but also to maintain that racial conflict and competition in the economic sector—the most important historical factors in the subjugation of blacks—have been substantially reduced. However, it could be argued that the firm white resistance to public school desegregation, residential integration, and black control of central cities all indicate the unyielding importance of race in America. The argument could even be entertained that the impressive occupational gains of the black middle class are only temporary and that as soon as affirmative action pressures are relieved, or as soon as the economy experiences a prolonged recession, industries will return to their old racial practices. Both of these arguments are compelling, if not altogether persuasive. Taking the latter contention first, there is little available evidence to suggest that the economic gains of privileged blacks will be reversed. Despite the fact that the recession of the early 1970s decreased job prospects for all educated workers, the more educated blacks continued to experience a faster rate of job advancement than their white counterparts.[2] And although it is always possible that an economic disaster could produce racial competition for higher-paying jobs and white efforts to exclude talented blacks, it is difficult to entertain this idea as a real possibility in the face of the powerful political and social movement against job discrimination. At this point there is every reason to believe that talented and educated blacks, like talented and educated whites, will continue to enjoy the advantages and privileges of their class status.

My response to the first argument is not to deny the current racial antagonism in the sociopolitical order but to suggest that such antagonism has far less effect on individual or group access to those opportunities and resources that are centrally important for life survival than antagonism in the economic sector. The factors that most severely affected black life-chances in previous years were the racial oppression and antagonism in the economic sector. As race declined in importance in the economic sector, the Negro class structure became more differentiated and black life chances became increasingly a consequence of class affiliation. Furthermore, it is even difficult to identify the form of racial contact in the sociopolitical order as the ultimate source of the manifestations of conflict between lower-income blacks and whites; because neither the degree of racial competition between the have-nots, nor their structural relations in urban communities, nor their patterns of interaction constitute the ultimate source of present racial antagonism. As this study suggests, the ultimate basis for current racial tension is the deleterious effect of basic structural changes in the modern American economy on black and white lower-income groups, changes that include uneven economic growth, increasing technology and automation, industry relocation, and labor-market segmentation.

The situation of marginality and redundancy created by the modern industrial society deleteriously affects all the poor, regardless of race. Underclass whites, Hispano-Americans, and native Americans all are victims, to a greater or lesser degree, of class subordination under advanced capitalism. It is true that blacks are disproportionately represented in the underclass population (of persons below the low-income level in 1974, 31 percent were black) and that about one-third of the entire black population is in the underclass. But the significance of these facts has more to do with the historical consequences of racial oppression than with the current effects of race. Although the percentage of blacks below the low-income level dropped steadily throughout the 1960s (from 55 in 1959 to 33.5 in 1970), one of the legacies of the racial oppression in previous years is the continued disporportionate black representation in the underclass. And since 1970 both poor whites and nonwhites have evidenced very little progress in their elevation from the ranks of the underclass.[3] In the final analysis, therefore, the challenge of economic dislocation in modern industrial society calls for public policy programs to attack inequality on a broad class front, policy programs, in other words, that go beyond the limits of ethnic and racial discrimination by directly confronting the pervasive and destructive features of class subordination.

NOTES

Chapter One

1. See, William J. Wilson, *Power, Racism and Privilege: Race Relations in Theoretical and Sociohistorical Perspectives* (New York: The Free Press, 1973).

2. In Marxist terminology, the "superstructure" refers to the arrangements of beliefs, norms, ideologies, and noneconomic institutions.

3. However, not all theorists who emphasize the importance of economic class in explanations of race relations simply relegate problems of race to the superstructure. The Marxist scholars Michael Burawoy and Eugene Genovese recognize the reciprocal influence between the economic class structure and aspects of the superstructure (belief systems, political systems, etc.), a position which I also share and which is developed more fully in subsequent sections of this chapter. See Eugene D. Genovese, *Roll, Jordan, Roll: The World the Slaves Made* (New York: Pantheon, 1974); idem, *In Red and Black: Marxian Explorations in Southern and Afro-American History* (New York: Vintage Press, 1971); and Michael Burawoy, "Race, Class, and Colonialism," *Social and Economic Studies* 23 (1974): 521–50.

4. Oliver C. Cox, *Caste, Class and Race: A Study in Social Dynamics* (Garden City, New York: Doubleday, 1948); Paul A. Baran and Paul M. Sweezy, *Monopoly Capital: An Essay on the American Economic and Social Order* (Harmondsworth: Penguin, 1966); Michael Reich, "The Economics of Racism," in *Problems in Political Economy*, ed. David M. Gordon (Lexington, Mass.: Heath, 1971); and M. Nikolinakos, "Notes on an Economic Theory of Racism," *Race: A Journal of Race and Group Relations* 14 (1973): 365–81.

5. Edna Bonacich, "A Theory of Ethnic Antagonism: The Split Labor Market," *American Sociological Review* 37 (October 1972): 547–59; idem, "Abolition, The Extension of Slavery and the Position of Free Blacks: A Study of Split Labor Markets in the United States," *American Journal of Sociology* 37 (1975): 601–28.

6. For examples of alternative and less orthodox Marxist explanations of race, see Eugene D. Genovese, *The Political Economy of Slavery: Studies in the Economy and Society of the Slave South* (New York: Pantheon, 1966); idem, *The World the Slave-*

holders Made: Two Essays in Interpretation (New York: Pantheon, 1969); idem, *In Red and Black*; idem, *Roll, Jordan, Roll*; and Burawoy, "Race, Class, and Colonialism."

7. "Exploitation," in Marxian terminology, refers to the difference between the wages workers receive and the value of the goods they produce. The size of this difference, therefore, determines the degree of exploitation.

8. Bonacich, "A Theory of Ethnic Antagonism," p. 557.

9. Ibid., p. 549.

10. Ibid., p. 553.

11. Ibid., p. 549.

12. Ibid., p. 555.

13. Ibid., p. 556.

14. Wilson, *Power, Racism, and Privilege*. For a discussion of social belief systems, see also John Rex, "The Concept of Race in Sociological Theory," in *Race and Racialism*, ed. Sami Zubaida (London: Tavistock Publications, 1970).

15. Rex, "The Concept of Race," p. 51.

16. Herbert Blumer, "Industrialisation and Race Relations," in *Industrialisation and Race Relations: A Symposium*, ed. Guy Hunter (London: Oxford University Press, 1965), pp. 200–253.

17. Ibid., p. 229.

18. Ibid., p. 232.

19. In Blumer's analysis, the bases of an established racial order are the continuous and clearly defined relations between two or more racial groups in a society. It follows, therefore, that new racial or ethnic immigrants could enter into the society and not be exposed to discriminatory treatment or not be sanctioned by racist norms until or unless they are perceived by certain segments of the dominant group as a competitive threat or as undesirable aliens.

20. Sheila T. Vander Horst, "The Effects of Industrialisation on Race Relations in South Africa," in *Industrialisation and Race Relations: A Symposium*, pp. 117–18.

21. Neil J. Smelser, *Karl Marx on Society and Social Change* (Chicago: University of Chicago Press, 1974), p. xiv. According to Smelser, Marx used the notions "forces of production" and "social relations of production" as constituting the "mode of production." However, in Marx's writings the mode of production is often discussed as equivalent only to the "forces of production." To avoid confusion, I have chosen the term "system of production" which denotes the interrelation of the forces of production and the mode of production.

22. Pierre L. van den Berghe, *Race and Racism: A Comparative Perspective* (New York: John Wiley and Sons, 1967), p. 26.

23. See, for example, Genovese, *Roll, Jordan, Roll.*

24. An exception to this pattern occurred in the cities of the antebellum South, where nonslaveholding whites played a major role in the development of urban segregation. However, since an overwhelming majority of the population resided in rural areas, race relations in the antebellum southern cities were hardly representative of the region. This point is discussed in greater detail in the next chapter.

25. van den Berghe, *Race and Racism,* p. 27.

26. Marvin Harris, *Patterns of Race in the Americas* (New York: Walker, 1964), p. 96.

27. Ibid., p. 96.

28. van den Berghe, *Race and Racism,* p. 28.

29. Nathan Glazer, "Blacks and Ethnic Groups: The Difference, and the Political Difference It Makes," in *Key Issues in the Afro-American Experience,* ed. Nathan I. Huggins, Martin Kilson, and Daniel M. Fox (New York: Harcourt Brace Jovanovich, 1971), 2: 209.

30. E. Franklin Frazier, *Black Bourgeoisie* (New York: The Free Press, 1957). See also Nathan Hare, *Black Anglo-Saxons* (New York: Collier, 1965).

31. The theoretical implications of this development for ethnic groups in general are discussed by Milton Gordon under the concept "ethclass." See Milton M. Gordon, *Assimilation in American Life* (New York: Oxford University Press, 1964).

Chapter Two

1. Kenneth M. Stampp, *The Peculiar Institution: Slavery in the Ante-Bellum South* (New York: Alfred A. Knopf, 1956), pp. 25–31.

2. Eugene D. Genovese, *Roll, Jordan, Roll: The World the Slaves Made* (New York: Pantheon Books, 1974), p. 27. I am indebted to Genovese (especially for part 1 of book 1, *Roll, Jordan, Roll*) for part of the discussion that follows.

3. Eric Foner, *Free Soil, Free Labor, Free Men: The Ideology of the Republican Party before the Civil War* (New York: Oxford University Press, 1970), p. 100.

4. Genovese, *Roll, Jordan Roll,* p. 32.

5. Sterling D. Spero and Abram L. Harris, *The Black Worker* (New York: Columbia University Press, 1931), p. 7.

6. Foner, *Free Soil, Free Labor, Free Men,* chap. 3.

7. Quoted in ibid., p. 89.

8. Ibid., p. 89.

9. Stanley M. Elkins, *Slavery: A Problem in American Institutional and Intellectual Life* (Chicago: University of Chicago Press, 1959); Genovese, *Roll, Jordan, Roll*; and Robert William Fogel and Stanley L. Engerman, *Time on the Cross: The Economics of American Negro Slavery* (Boston: Little, Brown, 1974), vol. 1.

10. Edmund S. Morgan, *American Slavery, American Freedom: The Ordeal of Colonial Virginia.* (New York: W. W. Norton, 1975).

11. The decline in the number of white indentured servants entering the colonies is possibly related to concern about the conditions that brought about the Bacon's Rebellion and the discontent expressed by servants following that disturbance. Also, Englishmen experienced less pressure to leave home by the third quarter of the century. "Complaints of overpopulation in England had ceased, as statesmen and political thinkers sought ways of putting the poor to work" (ibid., p. 299).

12. Ibid., pp. 297–98.

13. Ibid., p. 297. Also see George M. Frederickson, "Toward a Social Interpretation of the Development of American Racism," in *Key Issues in the Afro-American Experience*, vol. 1, ed. Nathan I. Huggins, Martin Kilson, and Daniel M. Fox (New York: Harcourt Brace Jovanovich, 1971).

14. Morgan, *American Slavery*, p. 312.

15. Quoted in ibid., pp. 312–13.

16. Ibid., p. 313.

17. Genovese, *Roll, Jordan, Roll*, p. 38.

18. Carl N. Degler, "The Irony of American Negro Slavery," in *Perspectives and Irony in American Slavery*, ed. Harry P. Owens (Jackson: University Press of Mississippi, 1976), p. 5.

19. Ibid., p. 6. In this connection, Degler comments that "It is possible that the slave trade was able to be closed only because natural increase had already demonstrated that it was capable of meeting the demand for new slaves. The source of this decision, however, is not as important as the fact that the exigencies of maintaining a slave system without additions from outside the country were such that the physical condition of the slaves had to be more than minimal. And from present knowledge of the law and the actual treatment of slaves in the colonial period and in the years of the nineteenth century after the closing of the slave trade, conditions did improve markedly, if gradually."

20. Genovese, *Roll, Jordan, Roll*; and Fogel and Engerman, *Time on the Cross.*

21. This fact alone leads one to question the relevance of Herbert G. Gutman's argument as far as the southern slave regime is concerned, namely, that "A high reproduction rate does not depend upon 'good treatment,'" and that "A detailed scholarly literature shows that diverse populations with very low standards increase rapidly." See Herbert G. Gutman, *The Black Family in Slavery and Freedom, 1750–1925* (New York: Pantheon, 1976), p. 310.

22. Genovese, *Roll, Jordan, Roll*, p. 57.

23. Fogel and Engerman, *Time on the Cross*, p. 5.

24. Ibid., p. 115.

25. Genovese, *Roll, Jordan, Roll*, pp. 59–60.

26. Ibid., p. 57.

27. W. E. B. DuBois, *Black Reconstruction* (New York: Harcourt, Brace and Co., 1935), p. 9.

28. John W. Blassingame, *The Slave Community: Plantation Life in the Ante-Bellum South* (New York: Oxford University Press, 1972), p. 160; and Edmund S. Morgan, *American Slavery*, chap. 15.

29. Elkins, *Slavery*. In response to his critics, Elkins now recognizes that his book did not give sufficient attention to the slave culture. On this point, he states: "The movement to explore black folk culture is in itself an exciting and salutary development which promises much in the way of lighting up the past. In the interests of conceptual mobility however, I wonder how exclusively it ought to be tied to the problem of resistance to slavery. The two are certainly related. But there should also be a way of allowing for the ebb and flow of folk culture over time, and of discovering whether there may be conditions under which such culture and the range of its expression flourishes, and other conditions which tend, relatively speaking, to inhibit it" ("The Social Consequences of Slavery," in *Key Issues in the Afro-American Experience*, 1:139. See also, Elkins, "On Slavery and Ideology," in Ann Lane, ed., *The Debate over Slavery: Stanley Elkins and His Critics* (Champaign: The University of Illinois Press, 1971), pp. 325–78.

30. See for example, the articles in Lane, ed. *Debate over Slavery*, especially the article by Roy Simon Bryce-Laporte, "Slaves as Inmates, Slaves as Men: A Sociological Discussion of Elkins' Thesis"; Blassingame, *The Slave Community*; Genovese,

Roll, Jordan, Roll; Fogel and Engerman, Time on the Cross; and
Gutman, The Black Family. For a good discussion of this research,
see the review-essay by George M. Fredrickson, "The Gutman
Report," The New York Review of Books, 23, no. 15 (September
30, 1976):18–22, 27.
   31. Genovese, Roll, Jordan Roll; and Gutman, The Black Family.
   32. Genovese, Roll, Jordan, Roll, pp. 3–7.
   33. Ibid., p. 658.
   34. Ibid., p. 7.
   35. Gutman, The Black Family, p. 309.
   36. Genovese, Roll, Jordan, Roll, pt. 1.
   37. Gutman, The Black Family, p. 310.
   38. Genovese, Roll, Jordan, Roll, p. 33.
   39. Ibid.
   40. In the discussion of urban slavery in the South, I am
heavily indebted to Richard C. Wade, Slavery in the Cities: The
South 1820–1860 (New York: Oxford University Press, 1964).
   41. Ibid., p. 48.
   42. Ibid., p. 75.
   43. Ibid., p. 277.
   44. Fogel and Engerman, Time on the Cross.

Chapter Three

   1. See Roger W. Shugg, Origins of Class Struggle in Louisiana
(Baton Rouge: Louisiana State University Press, 1939), pp. 88–89.
   2. Sterling D. Spero and Abram L. Harris, The Black Worker
(New York: Columbia University Press, 1931), pp. 5–9; Bernard
Mandel, Labor: Free and Slave; Workingmen and the Anti-Slavery
Movement in the United States (New York: Associated Authors,
1955), chap. 2; Robert William Fogel and Stanley L. Engerman
Time on the Cross: The Economics of American Negro Slavery
(Boston: Little, Brown, 1974), 1:38–43.
   3. Spero and Harris, The Black Worker, p. 9.
   4. Mandel, Labor.
   5. Ibid., p. 31.
   6. Herman Schluter, Labor and Slavery: A Chapter from the
Social History of America (New York: Socialist Literature Company, 1913), p. 92.
   7. Philip S. Foner, History of the Labor Movement in the
United States (New York: International Publishers, 1947), 1:260.

8. Spero and Harris, *The Black Worker*, pp. 7–11; Richard B. Morris, *Government and Labor in Early America* (New York: Octagon, 1965), pp. 186–88; Robert R. Russell, *Economic Aspects of Southern Sectionalism* (Urbana: University of Illinois Press, 1923), pp. 219–20; T. M. Whitfield, *Slavery Agitation in Virginia, 1792–1832* (Baltimore: Johns Hopkins University Press, 1930); Schluter, *Labor and Slavery*, 99–100; Foner, *Labor Movement in the U.S.*, pp. 258–64; and Robert S. Starobin, *Industrial Slavery in the Old South* (New York: Oxford University Press, 1970), pp. 211–12.

9. Morris, *Government and Labor*, pp. 185–86; and Foner, *Labor Movement in the U.S.*, p. 262.

10. Mandel, *Labor*, p. 49.

11. Schluter, *Labor and Slavery*, p. 96.

12. Mandel, *Labor*, p. 57.

13. Ibid., p. 57.

14. Cf. William J. Wilson, *Power, Racism and Privilege: Race Relations in Theoretical and Sociohistorical Perspectives* (New York: The Free Press, 1973), chap. 5.

15. Alexis de Tocqueville, *Democracy in America*, ed. J. P. Mayer (New York: Doubleday, 1969), p. 343.

16. Arthur Zilversmit, *The First Emancipation: The Abolition of Slavery in the North* (Chicago: The University of Chicago Press, 1967), p. 53.

17. Mandel, *Labor*, p. 61.

18. Morris, *Government and Labor*, p. 183.

19. W. E. B. Du Bois, *The Philadelphia Negro: A Social Study*, Political Economy and Public Law Series no. 14 (Boston: Ginn, 1899), p. 15; Mandel, *Labor*, p. 63.

20. Leon F. Litwack, *North of Slavery: The Negro in the Free States, 1790–1860* (Chicago: University of Chicago Press, 1961), pp. 5–6.

21. Mandel, *Labor*, p. 61; also see Williston Lofton, "Abolition and Labor," *The Journal of Negro History* 33 (July 1948):249–93.

22. Litwack, *North of Slavery*, p. 159.

23. Spero and Harris, *The Black Worker*, p. 12; also see Du Bois, *The Philadelphia Negro*, p. 33, and idem, *The Negro Artisan* (Atlanta: Atlanta University Press, 1902), pp. 15–16.

24. Herman D. Bloch, *The Circle of Discrimination: An Economic and Social Study of the Black Man in New York* (New York: New York University Press, 1969), p. 34. See also Litwack, *North of Slavery*, p. 166.

25. Litwack, *North of Slavery*, p. 166.

26. See Ira Berlin, *Slaves without Masters: The Free Negro in the Antebellum South* (New York: Pantheon Books, 1974), p. 136. Berlin points out that "The great mass of Negro freedmen lived in the tidewater of the Upper South between Delaware and North Carolina, where the post-Revolutionary manumission movement had flourished. Better than half the free Negroes in the South resided in Delaware, Maryland and Virginia" (p. 179).

27. Ibid., p. 28.

28. Eugene H. Berwanger, *The Frontier against Slavery: Western Anti-Negro Prejudice and the Slavery Extension Controversy* (Urbana: University of Illinois Press, 1967), p. 18.

29. Berwanger, *Frontier against Slavery*, and V. Jacque Voegeli, *Free but Not Equal: The Midwest and the Negro during the Civil War* (Chicago: University of Chicago Press, 1967); see also Emma Lou Thornbrough, *The Negro in Indiana before 1900: A Study of a Minority* (Indiana Historical Collections, vol. 37 Indianapolis: Indiana Historical Bureau, 1957).

30. Litwack, *North of Slavery*, p. 97.

31. See Albon P. Man, Jr., "Labor Competition and the New York Draft Riots of 1863," *The Journal of Negro History* 36 (October 1951):375–405; and Williston Loften, "Northern Labor and the Negro during the Civil War," *The Journal of Negro History* 34 (July 1949):251–73.

32. Spero and Harris, *The Black Worker*, p. 13.

33. Ibid., pp. 13–14; and Schluter, *Labor and Slavery*, pp. 34–84.

34. Oliver C. Cox, *Caste, Class and Race: A Study in Social Dynamics* (Garden City, New York: Doubleday, 1948).

35. Paul A. Baran and Paul M. Sweezy, *Monopoly Capital: An Essay on the American Economic and Social Order* (Harmondsworth: Penguin, 1966), p. 247.

36. C. Vann Woodward, *American Counterpoint: Slavery and Racism in the North-South Dialogue* (Boston: Little, Brown, 1971), p. 251.

37. Ibid., p. 252.

38. Benjamin Quarles, *The Negro in the Making of America* (New York: Collier Books, 1964), p. 131.

39. John Hope Franklin, *From Slavery to Freedom*, 3d ed. (New York: Alfred A. Knopf, 1967); and Peter M. Bergman, *The Chronological History of the Negro in America* (New York: Harper and Row, 1969).

40. E. Franklin Frazier, *The Negro in the United States* (New York: Macmillan, 1957). Frazier points out that "The planter and propertied classes did not fail to take advantage of the traditional prejudices of the poor whites and the competition between the latter and the Negro to destroy any cooperation between the two groups. The poor whites were constantly subjected to propaganda concerning supremacy and purity of the white race" (p. 135).

41. Ray Marshall, "Industrialisation and Race Relations in the Southern United States," in *Industrialisation and Race Relations*, ed. Guy Hunter (London: Oxford University Press, 1961), p. 66.

42. Woodward, *American Counterpoint*, p. 254.

43. C. Vann Woodward, *Origins of the New South, 1877–1913.* (Baton Rouge: Louisiana State University Press, 1951), pp. 254–55.

44. See Otis M. Scruggs, "The Economic and Racial Components of Jim Crow," in *Key Issues in the Afro-American Experience*, ed. Nathan I. Huggins, Martin Kilson, and Daniel M. Fox (New York: Harcourt Brace Jovanovich, 1971), pp. 70–87.

45. Ibid., p. 73.

46. Ibid.; Woodward, *Origins of the New South*; and V. O. Key, Jr., *Southern Politics in State and Nation* (New York: Alfred A. Knopf, 1949).

47. Scruggs, "Jim Crow," p. 81.

48. Woodward, *Origins of the New South*, pp. 211–12, and Scruggs, "Jim Crow," pp. 84–85.

49. Woodward, *Origins of the New South*, p. 211.

50. Quoted in ibid., p. 257.

51. Ibid., p. 257.

52. C. Vann Woodward, *Tom Watson: An Agrarian Rebel* (New York: Oxford University Press, 1938); Carmen J. Owens, "Power, Racism and Coalition Politics: A Re-examination of the Populist Movement in Georgia" (Master's thesis, University of Chicago, 1973); Bergman, *The Negro in America*, p. 310.

53. Franklin, *From Slavery to Freedom*, p. 337.

54. Commenting on the attitude of three of the most powerful Democratic leaders of the Deep South, Woodward states: "As late as 1879, three foremost spokesmen of the South, Lamar of Mississippi, Hampton of South Carolina, and Stephens of Georgia, agreed in a public statement that the disfranchisement of the Negro was not only impossible but undesired. Lamar declared that it was 'a political impossibility under any circumstances short of revolution,' and that even if it were possible the

South would not permit it. Hampton, who claimed the distinction of being 'the first man at the South' to advocate suffrage for the emancipated slave, remarked that the Negro 'naturally allies himself with the most conservative of the whites' " (*Origins of the New South*, p. 321).

55. Ibid., p. 324.

56. These procedures were so comprehensive that many poor whites were also disfranchised. This led some states in the South to initiate the so-called "grandfather clause," which waived the voting requirements for those citizens whose ancestors had voted in the 1860 election.

57. Cf. Donald Young, *American Minority Peoples: A Study in Racial and Cultural Conflicts in the United States* (New York: Harper, 1932), p. 99; and Fogel and Engerman, *Time on the Cross*, pp. 258–64.

58. Genovese, *Roll, Jordan, Roll.*

59. Franklin, *From Slavery to Freedom*, p. 439.

60. Some readers may take issue with what seems to be a process of mechanical allocation in the application of the economic class theories to different historical periods of American race relations. As pointed out by Professor Jan Dizard in private communication, it may be argued that either both theories are wrong (or are less parsimonious than another as yet unrealized theory) or that historical observation is incomplete, or both. My position is that the application of any given theory to a particular observable situation depends on whether the conditions under which the theory applies have in fact been met. If the conditions for the application of the theory are not present, it certainly does not mean that the theory is necessarily false. It only means that an adequate test of the theory's scope and validity cannot be made. Specification of the initial conditions for the application of a theory is therefore crucial. And this is exactly what I have in mind when I argue that meaningful application of the economic class theories depends on knowledge of the constraints imposed by the system of production (or even of the arrangement of the polity, as I pointed out in Chapter 1 and will more fully demonstrate in later chapters). Of course, for our purposes, it would be desirable to develop a more comprehensive theory that systematically integrates propositions concerning the role of the system of production with propositions drawn from the economic class theories. Although I do not attempt such an ambitious project in this book, I do believe that my theoretical argu-

ments have sufficient scope to deal with a variety of historical situations and constitute at least an implicit theory of social change and race relations.

Chapter Four

1. Allen Spear, "The Origins of the Urban Ghetto, 1870–1915," in *Key Issues in the Afro-American Experience*, ed. Nathan I. Huggins, Martin Kilson, and Daniel M. Fox (New York: Harcourt Brace Jovanovich, 1971), pp. 153–66.

2. Gilbert Osofsky, *Harlem: The Making of a Ghetto, 1830–1930* (New York: Harper, 1966), p. 36.

3. Ibid., pp. 36–37.

4. Spear, "Origins of the Urban Ghetto," p. 159.

5. Osofsky, *Harlem*, p. 36.

6. Spear, "Origins of the Urban Ghetto," p. 159.

7. Ibid.

8. Osofsky, *Harlem*, pp. 41–42.

9. Sterling D. Spero and Abram L. Harris, *The Black Worker* (New York: Columbia University Press, 1931), p. 132.

10. Gunnar Myrdal, *An American Dilemma: The Negro Problem and Modern Democracy* (New York: Harper and Row, 1944), p. 191.

11. Ibid.

12. Ibid., p. 193.

13. Donald Young, *American Minority Peoples: A Study in Racial and Cultural Conflicts in the United States* (New York: Harper, 1932).

14. Chicago Commission on Race Relations, *The Negro in Chicago: A Study of Race Relations and a Race Riot* (Chicago: University of Chicago Press, 1922).

15. The source for these figures on the changing urban black population is Hollis R. Lynch, *The Black Urban Condition: A Documentary History, 1866–1971* (New York: Thomas Y. Crowell, 1973), p. 427.

16. Myrdal, *An American Dilemma*, p. 193.

17. Ibid., p. 252.

18. Ibid., chap. 12; see also Reynolds Farley, *Growth of the Black Population: A Study of Demographic Trends* (Chicago: Markham Publishing Co., 1970).

19. Richard H. Day, "Technological Change and the Share-cropper," *American Economic Review* 57 (June 1967):429.

20. Daniel R. Fusfeld, *The Basic Economics of the Urban Racial Crisis* (New York: Holt, Rinehart and Winston, 1973), p. 16.

21. Michael J. Piore, "Negro Workers in the Mississippi Delta: Problems of Displacement and Adjustment," *Proceedings of the Industrial Research Association* (Winter, 1967), pp. 366–67.

22. Edna Bonacich, "Advanced Capitalism and Black-White Relations in the United States: A Split Labor Market Interpretation," *American Sociological Review* 41 (February 1976):34–51.

23. Spear, "Origins of the Urban Ghetto," p. 163.

24. Spero and Harris, *The Black Worker*, p. 152.

25. Ibid., pp. 155–56.

26. Cf. William Z. Foster, *The Great Steel Strike and Its Lessons* (New York: Da Capo Press, 1971), p. 211.

27. Elliott M. Rudwick, *Race Riot at East St. Louis* (Carbondale: Southern Illinois University Press, 1964), pp. 16–17.

28. Spero and Harris, *The Black Worker*, p. 208; Bonacich, "Advanced Capitalism and Black-White Relations in the United States," p. 41; and Alma Herbst, "The Negro in the Slaughtering and Meat Packing Industry in Chicago" (Ph.D. dissertation, University of Chicago, 1930), p. 33.

29. Bonacich, "Advanced Capitalism and Black-White Relations in the United States," p. 42.

30. Spero and Harris, *The Black Worker*, p. 140.

31. Rudwick, *Race Riot*, p. 219 .

32. Ibid., p. 217; Chicago Commission on Race Relations, *The Negro in Chicago*, chap 1; National Advisory Commission on Civil Disorders, *Report of the National Advisory Commission on Civil Disorders* (New York: Bantam Books, 1968), p. 218.

33. I emphasize the word "interracial" because these outbreaks were qualitatively different from the ghetto revolts of the 1960s. The earlier interracial riots involved groups of black citizens attacked by and retaliating against groups of white citizens, whereas the later ghetto revolts involved groups of blacks attacking white symbols or white agents located in the black community. Unlike in the interracial confrontations up to 1943, the white citizenry were rarely identified as combatants in the later ghetto revolts. Although the first major ghetto revolt occurred in Harlem in 1943, the ghetto riot emerged as a pattern of racial violence mainly in the advanced industrial stage of race relations, as we shall see in Chapter 6. For a discussion of the difference between interracial riots and ghetto revolts, see William J. Wilson, "Race Relations Models and Ghetto Behavior," in *Nation of Nations: The Ethnic Experience and the Racial Crisis*, ed. Peter I.

Rose (New York: Random House, 1975), pp. 259–77; and, Morris Janowitz, "Patterns of Collective Racial Violence," in *Violence in America: Historical and Comparative Perspectives*, ed. Hugh Davis Graham and Ted Robert Gurr (New York: Bantam Books, 1969), pp. 412–44.

34. Rudwick, *Race Riot*, pp. 217–18.

35. For a good discussion of the "longstanding discord between white and black competitors in the Chicago labor market" as the major cause of the 1919 race riot in that city, see William M. Tuttle, Jr., "Labor Conflict and Racial Violence: The Black Worker in Chicago, 1894–1919," *Labor History* 10 (Summer 1969): 408–32.

36. For example, Ray Marshall points out that from 1920 to 1933 the American Federation of Labor's union membership declined from 4,700,000 to 2,100,000. However, part of this sharp decline was undoubtedly due to the effect of the depression in the early 1930s. Ray Marshall, *The Negro and Organized Labor* (New York: John Wiley and Sons, 1965), p. 22.

37. Ibid, pp. 22–23.

38. Ibid, pp. 34–35; and Bonacich, "Advanced Capitalism and Black-White Relations in the United States," p. 45.

39. Marshall, *The Negro and Organized Labor*, p. 35.

40. Ray Marshall, *The Negro Worker* (New York: Random House, 1967), p. 24.

41. As Spero and Harris stated, the psychology of craft unions generated the atmosphere of an "exclusive club, consisting of those who now belong. The smaller it is kept the higher will be the value of the craftman's service. It is therefore made as difficult as possible for new members to join. If whole classes, such as Negroes, can be automatically excluded, the problem of keeping the membership down is made that much easier" (*The Black Worker*, pp. 461–62).

42. August Meier and Elliott Rudwick, *From Plantation to Ghetto: An Interpretive History of the American Negro*, rev. ed. (New York: Hill and Wang, 1970), p. 242.

43. For the arguments developed in this section, I am heavily indebted to Martin Kilson's "Black Politicians: A New Power," *Dissent* (August 1971):333–45; and idem, "Political Change in the Negro Ghetto, 1900–1940's," in *Key Issues in the Afro-American Experience*, ed. Nathan I. Huggins, Martin Kilson, and Daniel M. Fox (New York: Harcourt Brace Jovanovich, 1971); and Ira Katznelson, *Black Men, White Cities: Race, Politics and Migration in the United States, 1900–30, and Britain, 1948–68* (Lon-

don: Oxford University Press, 1973), esp. chap. 7. Parts of this
section were originally presented as a paper entitled "The Application of the Colonial Model to the Black Community" (Vernon
Gray, coauthor), read at the annual meeting of the American
Sociological Association, August 1971, Denver, Colorado.

44. Cf. Herbert J. Gans, "The Ghetto Rebellions and Urban
Class Conflict," in Robert Connery, ed., Urban Riots (New York:
Proceedings of Academy of Political Science, 1969), vol. 1, no.
1; and Kilson, "Black Politicians, A New Power," p. 334.

45. Katznelson, Black Men, White Cities, p. 111.

46. Ibid., p. 112.

47. Ibid., p. 113. The one notable exception to this general
pattern was in Chicago, where the small and ethnically homo-
geneous political wards enabled blacks to develop an organized,
territorially based submachine directly linked to the party headquarters through the decentralized political structure. Nonetheless, the South Side black machine in Chicago was little more
than an extension or appendage of the white party organization.
See Katznelson, Black Men, White Cities, chap. 6.

48. Kilson, "Black Politics: A New Power," p. 336.

49. Ibid., p. 337.

50. See, for example, Spero and Harris, The Black Worker, and
Bonacich, "Advanced Capitalism and Black-White Race Relations
in the United States," pp. 36–37; and Ira De A. Reid, Negro
Membership in American Labor Unions (New York: Negro Universities Press, 1969), p. 17. The studies by Reid and by Spero and
Harris present data that indicate a lower wage-rate for blacks
than whites for essentially the same work in southern industries.
The situation in the North was more complicated. In describing
the northern wage pattern, Bonacich states: "Blacks and whites
doing the same work in the same plant rarely were paid different
wages. But a wage differential appears in two more disguised
forms. First, as in the South, one finds racial segregation by job
title, with 'black' jobs generally paying less. For example, a steel
foundry in Chicago employing 135 people in 1917, 35 of whom
were black, paid white workers an average of $37 a week and
black workers an average of $29. . . . Such discrepancies are
typical and generally accounted for by the fact that blacks were
concentrated in unskilled and semi-skilled jobs; but job classi-
fications are sometimes arbitrary and a 'skill' may require very
little training. For example, Bailer points out that before World
War II only 10 percent of jobs in the automobile industry required more than one year of training or experience.

"The second indirect form of wage differential appears in segregation by firm, i.e., black workers are employed by firms which pay a lower wage rate than firms employing white workers even though they may be engaged in the same work" (Bonacich, "Advanced Capitalism and Black-White Race Relations in the U.S.," pp. 36–37).

51. David Brody, Steelworkers in America: The Nonunion Era (Cambridge: Harvard University Press, 1960), p. 186.

52. Young, American Minority Peoples, pp. 125–30.

53. Cf. William J. Wilson, "The Significance of Social and Racial Prisms," in Through Different Eyes: Black and White Perspectives on American Race Relations, ed. Peter I. Rose, Stanley Rothman, and William J. Wilson (New York: Oxford University Press, 1973).

54. On the other hand, some industrial unions in the early twentieth century were strong enough in labor-management relations to ignore black workers. The American Federation of Railway Workers, an independent union, and the Railway Carmen Union, an affiliate of the American Federation of Labor, were able to exclude blacks at the same time the CIO and the United Mine Workers were taking positive steps to organize them. In the final analysis, the more vulnerable a labor union was to employer exploitation, the more likely that black workers were accepted as members.

55. Katznelson, Black Men, White Cities, p. 117. On this point, Katznelson states: "In the machine period, when the party organizations provided the best access routes to positions of political control and mobility, blacks were on the periphery of party affairs. Furniss has calculated that blacks in 1910 had secured only 5 percent of the top patronage positions in New York City, proportional to their population (100 percent would indicate that their proportion of patronage positions equalled their proportion of the city's population); as late as 1930, they had secured under 20 percent of the positions at the top to which they were entitled by reference to the size of the population. By contrast, Italians— who in this period fared least well among the European ethnics —in 1930 controlled 27 percent of the higher echelon jobs they were entitled to by reference to their population" (p. 117).

56. Cf. Harry A. Bailey, Jr., "Negro Interest Group Strategies," Urban Affairs Quarterly 4 (September 1968):27–38.

57. See Henry L. Moon, Balance of Power: The Negro Vote (Garden City, New York: Doubleday, 1948).

58. As I reported in a previous publication, "President Truman, overwhelmingly picked by political observers to lose the Presidential election to Governor Dewey of New York recognized that he could not possibly defeat his Republican rival without the support of black Americans. For the first time since Reconstruction, the status of the black man was a central issue in a Presidential campaign, and much to the chagrin of its Southern members, the Democratic party in 1948 adopted a civil rights plank as part of its party platform. That same year, President Truman issued an executive order banning racial segregation in the Armed Forces —satisfying a demand originally introduced by black leaders in 1940. Such actions proved to be effective. Truman with the overwhelming support of black voters, narrowly defeated Dewey" (William J. Wilson, *Power, Racism and Privilege: Race Relations in Theoretical and Sociohistorical Perspectives* [New York: The Free Press, 1973], p. 123).

59. For a detailed discussion of blacks holding elected office, see James E. Conyers and Walter L. Wallace, *Black Elected Officials: A Study of Black Americans Holding Governmental Office* (New York: Russell Sage Foundation, 1976).

60. Katznelson, *Black Men, White Cities,* p. 118. The one notable exception to the nationwide demise of political machines is the Democratic machine in Chicago, whose old-style party organization has survived. For a good discussion of why the political power structure of Chicago has changed very little since the days of machine politics, see Harold F. Gosnell, *Machine Politics: Chicago Model,* 2d. ed. (Chicago: University of Chicago Press, 1968), pp. 221–38.

61. Bailey, "Negro Interest Group Strategies," p. 34.

62. Kilson, "Black Politics: A New Power," pp. 339–40.

Chapter Five

1. Charles C. Killingsworth, Jr., *Jobs and Income for Negroes* (Ann Arbor: University of Michigan Press, 1968), p. 11.

2. Ibid. It could be argued, however, that the favorable ratio of black/white unemployment reported in the 1930 and 1940 federal census reports is partly a statistical artifact. If we apply a measure for underutilized labor associated with seasonal work such as sharecropping and tenancy, work in which blacks were heavily concentrated in the 1920s and 1930s, then it could be argued that since the mid-1950s, the movement of blacks out of agriculture has resulted in the disguised unemployment of the

agricultural peonage being replaced by the undisguised unemployment of the urban subproletariat. This explanation is hardly sufficient, however, to explain the stability of the black/white unemployment ratio since the mid-1950s and the sharp increase in the black teenage unemployment rate beginning in the late sixties.

3. These figures for black youths are based on those computed for "blacks and other races" in which about 90 percent are black. However, in 1973, the U.S. Department of Labor began to collect data on blacks alone; when this is done, the official unemployment rates for blacks (adults and teenagers) actually increase. In the case of teenagers, the black unemployment rate increases from 32.9 percent to 34.9 percent in 1974, and the black/white teenage employment ratio increases from 2.4 to 2.5.

4. Congress of the United States, *The Unemployment of Nonwhite Americans*, Background Paper no. 11 (Washington, D.C.: Congressional Budget Office, July 19, 1976). The 1976 unemployment figures for blacks are based on those computed for "black and other races."

5. U.S. Department of Labor, *Manpower Report of the President* (Washington, D.C.: Government Printing Office, 1972), p. 85.

6. These figures are based on U.S. Department of Labor, *Handbook of Labor Statistics* 1975 (Washington, D.C.: Government Printing Office, 1975).

7. U.S. Department of Labor, *Manpower Report of the President* (Washington, D.C.: Government Printing Office, 1971), p. 85.

8. Some observers associate the rise of teenage unemployment with the introduction of minimum wage legislation. However, empirical studies on this subject have reached conflicting conclusions. In one of the most comprehensive studies on the subject, the Bureau of Labor Statistics concluded that, although the Fair Labor Standards Act (FLSA) may have helped to increase the unemployment of youth, it was difficult to separate its influence from the effects of several other factors such as the increase in the teenage population and the military draft. However, a study by Thomas Gale Moore reports that either an extension in coverage or an increase in the level or minimum wage produce a rise in teenage joblessness; and that black teenage joblessness was more affected by FLSA changes than was white teenage joblessness. However, Moore failed to account for the increased proportion of all youths in the labor force. Another study by

Masanore Hashimoto and Jacob Mincer reported no statistically significant unemployment effects from FLSA after accounting for the large increase in the teenage population. Finally, a study by Marvin Kosters and Finis Welch found that teenage unemployment was more vulnerable to cyclical fluctuations and that the teenage share of total employment was decreased when the minimum wage was increased. However, the authors of this study failed to take into account factors which could have effected teenage employment such as school enrollments and population growth.

After reviewing the findings of these studies, the economist Andrew Brimmer concluded that: "It is difficult to draw firm conclusions from these empirical studies unless one is willing to play one methodology off against another. On balance, however, I think the evidence tentatively suggests that changes in the FLSA may have had some adverse impact on teenage employment— especially through the extension of FLSA coverage to service and trade establishments with amendments in 1961 and 1966." See U.S. Bureau of Labor Statistics, "Youth Unemployment and Minimum Wages," Bulletin 1657, 1970; Thomas Gale Moore, "The Effects of Minimum Wages on Teenage Unemployment Rates," *Journal of Political Economy* 79 (July/August 1971); Masanore Hashimoto and Jacob Mincer, "Employment and Unemployment Effects of Minimum Wages," *The NBER Report on Research in Labor Markets for USLD* (New York: National Bureau of Economic Research, 1972); and Marvin Kosters and Finis Welch, "The Effects of Minimum Wages by Race, Sex and Age," in *Racial Discrimination in Economic Life*, ed. Anthony Pascal (Lexington, Mass.: Lexington Books, 1972). For a critical discussion of this literature, to which I am indebted, see Andrew F. Brimmer, "Employment and Income in the Black Community: Trends and Outlook," paper presented under the joint sponsorship of the Committee on Public Lectures, the Department of Economics, and the Institute of Government and Public Affairs at the University of California at Los Angeles, California, March 2, 1973.

9. U.S. Dept. of Labor, *Manpower Report of the President* (1972), p. 85.

10. See Killingsworth, *Jobs and Income for Negroes*, for a fuller discussion of this problem.

11. U.S. Dept. of Labor, *Manpower Report of the President* (1971), p. 85.

12. See John F. Kain, "The Distribution and Movement of Jobs and Industry," in *The Metropolitan Enigma: Inquiries into the*

Nature and Dimension of America's "Urban Crisis," ed. James Q. Wilson (Cambridge: Harvard University Press, 1968), p. 3; U.S. Dept. of Labor, *Manpower Report of the President* (1971), p. 88; and Raymond C. Hummel and John M. Nagel, *Urban Education in America: Problems and Prospects* (New York: Oxford University Press, 1973), p. 214.

13. Another factor that has probably had some effect on employment in northern central cities has been the relocation of goods-producing industries to "cheap labor" areas of the South. This has been particularly true of the meat-packing industry, which has traditionally been one of the major industrial employers of blacks. Also, some industries have left central cities and relocated overseas in search of cheaper labor. For a discussion of the effects of internal relocation on black workers, see Edna Bonacich, "Advanced Capitalism and Black-White Race Relations in the United States: A Split Labor Market Interpretation," *American Sociological Review* 41 (February 1976):34–51; and Walter A. Fogel, *The Negro in the Meat-Packing Industry* (Philadelphia: The University of Pennsylvania Press, 1970). For a discussion of the importance of external relocation, see Louis Turner, *Multinational Corporations and the Third World* (New York: Hill and Wang, 1973), chap. 7.

14. See Daniel Bell, *The Coming of Post-Industrial Society: A Venture in Social Forecasting* (New York: Basic Books, 1973), p. 132.

15. The association of white-collar jobs with the growing service-producing sector of American society is not to overlook the fact that there are blue-collar and white-collar positions in both the service and goods-producing sectors of the economy. However, even in the goods-producing sector, the proportion of blue-collar jobs is losing ground to white-collar positions. Daniel Bell has commented on this situation: "The spread of services, particularly in trade, finance, education, health and government, conjures up the picture of a white-collar society. But all services are not white-collar, since they include transportation workers and auto repairmen. But then, not all manufacturing is blue-collar. In 1970, the white-collar component within manufacturing —professional, managerial, clerical, and sales—came to almost 31 percent of the work force, while 69 percent were blue-collar workers (6,055,000 white-collar and 13,400,000 blue-collar). By 1975, the white-collar component will reach 34.5 percent. Within the blue-collar force itself, there has been a steady and distinct shift from direct production to non-production jobs, as more and

more work becomes automated and in the factory, workers increasingly are employed in machine-tending, repairs, and maintenance, rather than on the assembly line" (ibid., p. 133).

16. U.S. Dept. of Labor, *Manpower Report of the President* (1971), p. 91.

17. Charles C. Killingsworth, Jr., "The Continuing Labor Market Twist," *Monthly Labor Review* 91 (September 1968):12–17.

18. Ibid. p. 12.

19. Ibid.

20. U. S. Bureau of the Census, "The Social and Economic Status of the Black Population in the United States," *Current Population Reports*, Series P-23, no. 54 (1974), p. 52.

21. Peter B. Doeringer and Michael J. Piore, *Internal Labor Markets and Manpower Analysis*, Report submitted to the Office of Manpower Research, U.S. Dept. of Labor, 1970, chap. 8, pp. 2–3.

22. In parts of the following analysis, I am heavily indebted to James O'Connor's insightful study, *The Fiscal Crisis of the State* (New York: St. Martin's Press, 1973), and to Robert T. Averitt, *The Dual Economy* (New York: Norton, 1968). I have also benefited from the vast and growing literature on the dual labor market, especially Harold Baron and Bennet Hymer, "The Negro in the Chicago Labor Market," in Julius Jacobsen, ed., *The Negro and the American Labor Movement* (New York: Doubleday, Anchor Books, 1968); Barry Bluestone, "Low Wage Industries and the Working Poor," *Poverty and Human Resources Abstracts* 3 (March–April, 1968); Barry Bluestone, "The Tripartite Economy: Labor Markets and the Working Poor," *Poverty and Human Resources* 5 (July–August 1970); Peter B. Doeringer and Michael J. Piore, "Unemployment and the Dual Labor Market," *The Public Interest* 38 (Winter 1975); Peter B. Doeringer and Michael J. Piore, "Equal Employment Opportunity in Boston," *Industrial Relations* 9 (May 1970); Peter B. Doeringer and Michael J. Piore, *Internal Labor Markets and Manpower Analysis*; Peter B. Doeringer, ed., *Programs to Employ the Disadvantaged* (Englewood Cliffs, N.J.: Prentice-Hall, 1969); Louis A. Ferman, "The Irregular Economy: Informal Work Patterns in the Ghetto" (University of Michigan, mimeograph, 1977); David M. Gordon, *Theories of Poverty and Underemployment* (Lexington, Mass.: D.C. Heath, 1972); Michael J. Piore, "On the Job Training in the Dual Labor Market," in Arnold Weber et al., *Public-Private Manpower Policies* (Madison, Wis.: Industrial Relations Research Association, 1969); Michael J. Piore, "The Dual Labor Market: Theory and Im-

plications," in David M. Gordon, ed., *Problems in Political Economy; An Urban Perspective* (Lexington, Mass.: D.C. Heath, 1971); Thomas Vietorisz and Bennet Harrison, *The Economic Development of Harlem* (New York: Praeger, 1970); Howard M. Wachtel, "The Impact of Labor Market Conditions on Hard-Core Unemployment: A Case Study of Detroit," *Poverty and Human Resources* 5 (July–August 1970); U.S. Dept. of Labor, *Manpower Report of the President* (1971), pp. 96–99; and Michael L. Wachter, "Primary and Secondary Labor Markets: A Critique of the Dual Approach," *Brookings Papers on Economic Activity* 4 (1974): 637–81.

23. However, as O'Connor points out, "Low-seniority workers and many in unskilled and semi-skilled jobs are frequently little better off than their counterparts in competitive industries. For example, steelworkers with less than two years service are ineligible for supplementary unemployment benefits" (*Fiscal Crisis of the State*, p. 16).

24. For a more detailed discussion of employment patterns and the growth of the corporate sector, see O'Connor, *Fiscal Crisis of the State*. Also see Tom Kahn, "Problems of the Negro Movement," *Dissent* (Winter 1964):108–38; and Sidney M. Wilhelm, *Who Needs the Negro?* (Cambridge, Mass.: Schenkman Publishing Co., 1970).

25. Stanley L. Friedlander, *Unemployment in the Urban Core* (New York: Praeger, 1972); and U.S. Dept. of Labor, *Manpower Report of the President* (1971, p. 94. Also see Alice Handsaker Kidder, "Racial Difference in Job Search and Wages," *Monthly Labor Review* 91 (July 1968);24–26.

26. Friedlander, *Unemployment*, p. 119.

27. Averitt, *The Dual Economy*.

28. Edna Bonacich, "A Theory of Ethnic Antagonism: The Split Labor Market," *American Sociological Review* 37 (October 1972); "Abolition, the Extension of Slavery and the Position of Free Blacks: A Study of Split Labor Markets in the United States 1830–1863," *American Journal of Sociology* 81 (November 1975); "Advanced Capitalism and Black-White Relations in the United States: A Split Labor Market Interpretation."

29. U.S. Government, *Economic Report of the President* (Washington, D.C.: Government Printing Office, 1975), p. 113. This report points out that "Empirical studies have estimated the extent to which differences in State laws requiring 'equal pay for equal work' (prior to the national Civil Rights Act of 1964) affect race differences in income and unemployment, when other eco-

nomic variables are held constant. The results indicate that State equal pay laws reduced the gap between the wage rates of equally skilled blacks and whites but increased the difference in unemployment" (p. 113).

30. Cf. Kahn, "Problems of the Negro Movement," pp. 126–30.

31. Moreover, even the lower-level clerical positions tend to have higher pay scales than the operative, labor, and service-worker jobs. This is true for black and white workers. For example, whereas the median incomes in 1973 for black male operatives, service workers and laborers were $6,539, $4,562, and $4,052 respectively, the median income for black clerical and kindred workers was $8,007. These figures, of course, are based on wage scales in both the private and government sectors. U.S. Bureau of the Census, "The Social and Economic Status of the Black Population in the United States," 1974, *Current Population Reports*, Series P-23, no. 54 (Washington, D.C.: Government Printing Office, July 1975), p. 80.

32. Kahn, "Problems of the Negro Movement," pp. 128–29.

33. Richard B. Freeman, "Changes in the Labor Market for Black Americans, 1948–1972," *Brookings Papers on Economic Activity*, 1971, vol. 1, p. 100. A number of economists have attempted to research the effect of government antidiscrimination programs on the labor-market status of blacks. The research is not conclusive, as the studies present conflicting findings on the impact of government programs. The focus of much of this research has been on wage differentials, and the investigators have tended to obscure the significantly different relationship between antidiscrimination programs and the labor-market experience of low-wage blacks on the one hand, and high-wage blacks on the other. Thus the gains enjoyed by the high-wage blacks are offset by the decline in labor force participation rates and the increase in unemployment rates among low-wage blacks. Moreover, since many of these studies restrict their research to the private sector, they do not deal with the increase in black occupational gains in the government sector (especially state and local government employment). Finally, these studies do not account for the normative pressures to protect civil rights of minorities that were generated in large measure by the civil rights legislation of the 1960s. These pressures could affect the hiring practices of private and public industries, regardless of their receipt (or anticipated receipt) of government contracts with affirmative action stipulations.

For an excellent review of current economic research on the impact of the government on the labor-market status of blacks, see Richard Butler and James Heckman, *Equal Rights and Indus-*

trial Relations (Madison, Wisconsin: Industrial Relations Research Association, 1977).

34. Richard B. Freeman, *The Over-Educated American* (New York: Academic Press, 1976), pp. 141–42.

35. U.S. Bureau of the Census, "The Social and Economic Status of the Black Population in the United States, 1974," p. 57. Despite these occupational gains, the economic position of all black male graduates did not improve enough to reach equality in employment possibilities or in income with white males. "This is because the labor market is not a structureless locus in which persons of different ages are interchangeable units of labor. Just as young college graduates were more (negatively) affected by the market downturn than experienced personnel, young black men were more (positively) affected by the decline in market discrimination than their elders. Older black college men lacked the relevant training or managerial experience to take advantage of new opportunities and advanced only moderately in the new job market. One unfortunate consequence of this is that even though income discrimination has been eliminated for new entrants, the legacy of past discrimination is likely to maintain a sizeable black-white gap among college men as a whole for many years to come" (Freeman, *The Over-Educated American*, pp. 142–43).

36. Morris Janowitz, *Social Control of the Welfare State* (New York: Elsevier, 1976), p. xvii.

37. See O'Connor, *Fiscal Crisis of the State*, for a more detailed discussion of this process, esp. chap. 6.

38. On the basis of data reported in the 1970 United States census, the median earnings of black government workers in nonagricultural industries was 29 percent higher than the median earning of black workers in the private sector. See U.S. Bureau of the Census, *Census of the Population 1970*, Subject Reports, Industrial Characteristics, Table 44.

39. U.S. Bureau of the Census, "The Social and Economic Status of the Black Population in the United States, 1974," p. 97.

40. I am indebted to Katherine O'Sullivan See for bringing the data on education by occupational level to my attention. For a discussion of the implications of these changes for urban education, see William J. Wilson and Katherine O'Sullivan See, "School Desegregation and Structural Changes in the Economy," (Paper presented at the annual meeting of the American Sociological Association, New York City, August 30, 1976).

41. Doeringer and Piore, *Internal Labor Markets and Manpower Analysis*, pp. 5–6.

42. Daniel R. Fusfeld, *The Basic Economics of the Urban Racial Crisis* (New York: Holt, Rinehart and Winston, 1973), p. 31.

43. Stanley Friedlander, *Unemployment*; Doeringer and Piore, "Equal Employment Opportunity in Boston."

44. Elliot Liebow, *Tally's Corner: A Study of Streetcorner Men* (Boston: Little, Brown 1967), pp. 29–71; Leonard Reissman, "Readiness to Succeed: Mobility Aspirations and Modernism Among the Poor," *Urban Affairs Quarterly* (March, 1969):379–95; U.S. Dept. of Labor, *Manpower Report of the President* (1971), p. 107; and Doris Wilkinson and Ronald L. Taylor, eds., *The Black Male in America: Perspectives on His Status in Contemporary Society* (Chicago: Nelson-Hall Publishers, 1977).

45. Liebow, *Tally's Corner*, pp. 50–51.

46. Ibid. p. 59.

47. *Chicago Tribune*, January 29, 1976, sec. 7.

48. For good detail on this point, see Janowitz, *Social Control of the Welfare State.*

49. Peter B. Doeringer, ed., "Low-Income Labor Markets and Urban Manpower Programs: A Critical Assessment," Report submitted to the Office of Manpower Research, United States Department of Labor, January 1969.

50. Friedlander, *Unemployment*, p. 187.

51. Ibid. See also U.S. Dept. of Labor, *Manpower Report of the President* (1971), pp. 98–99.

52. U.S. Dept. of Labor, *Manpower Report of the President* (1974), p. 95. The six metropolitan areas include New York, N.Y., Philadelphia, Pa., Washington, D.C., Chicago, Ill., Detroit, Mich., and Los Angeles–Long Beach, Calif.

53. Ibid., p. 95.

54. U. S. Department of Commerce, "The Social and Economic Characteristics of the Black Population in the United States, 1973," Current Population Reports, Special Studies Series P-23, Washington, D.C.: U. S. Government Printing Office, 1957, p. 57.

55. Advisory Commission on Intergovernmental Relations, *Urban American and the Federal System* (Washington, D.C., 1969), M-47, p. 10.

56. Ibid., pp. 10–11.

57. See Ira Katznelson, "The Crisis of the Capitalist City: Urban Politics and Social Control," in *Theoretical Perspectives on Urban Politics*, ed. Willis D. Hawley and Michael Lipsky (Englewood Cliffs, N.J.: Prentice-Hall, 1976), p. 219; and David Gordon, "Income and Welfare in New York City," *The Public Interest* (Summer 1969).

58. Hummel and Nagle, *Urban Education*, pp. 202–3.

59. U.S. Dept. of Labor, *Manpower Report of the President* (1971), p. 92.

60. Ibid.

61. Advisory Commission on Intergovernmental Relations, *Urban America and the Federal System*, p. 10.

62. Friedlander, *Unemployment*, pp. 119–20.

63. Kahn, "Problems of the Negro Movement," p. 118.

64. Quoted by Paul Welks, "The White Ethnics," in *Through Different Eyes: Black and White Perspectives on American Race Relations*, ed. Peter I. Rose, Stanley Rothman, and William J. Wilson (New York: Oxford University Press, 1973), p. 172.

65. Ibid.

66. Murray Friedman, "The Jews," in *Through Different Eyes*, pp. 148–65.

67. Quoted in Friedman, *Unemployment*, pp. 153–54.

68. The exception are the attempts to desegregate public schools in the late nineteenth century. See August Meier and Elliott Rudwick, *From Plantation to Ghetto*, rev. ed. (New York: Hill and Wang, 1970).

69. U. S. Bureau of the Census, "The Social and Economic Characteristics of the Black Population in the United States, 1974," p. 153.

70. Richard A. Cloward and Frances Fox Piven, *The Politics of Turmoil: Poverty, Race, and the Urban Crisis* (New York: Vintage Books, 1975), p. 250.

71. See, for example, Freeman, "Changes in the Labor Market for Black Americans, 1948–72," pp. 67–120. Freeman associates the narrowing in the black-white wage differentials since the mid-sixties with the emergence of federal antidiscrimination programs. However, as Butler and Heckman have shown, Freeman's use of wage differentials does not reflect the relative reduction of Negro workers from the labor force, a reduction that was particularly prevalent among prime-age males, most of whom, it is reasonable to assume, were low-wage workers. See Butler and Heckman, *Equal Rights and Industrial Relations*.

Chapter Six

1. Eugene Genovese, *Roll, Jordan, Roll: The World the Slaves Made* (New York: Pantheon, 1974), pp. 587–97.

2. Leon F. Litwack, *North of Slavery: The Negro in the Free States, 1790–1860* (Chicago: The University of Chicago Press, 1961), pp. viii–ix.

3. See Sterling D. Spero and Abram L. Harris, *The Black Worker*. New York: Columbia University Press, 1931.

4. Allan Spear, "The Origins of the Urban Ghetto, 1870–1915," in *Key Issues in the Afro-American Experience*, ed. by Nathan I. Huggins, Martin Kilson, and Daniel M. Fox (New York: Harcourt Brace Jovanovich), p. 165.

5. Ibid.

6. Ibid.

7. Ibid. p. 166.

8. John Hope Franklin, *From Slavery to Freedom*, 3d ed (New York: Alfred A. Knopf, 1967), p. 496.

9. Leslie H. Fishel, Jr., and Benjamin Quarles, *The Negro American: A Documentary History* (Glenview, Ill.: Scott, Foresman, 1967), pp. 448–49.

10. Bayard Rustin, *The Foundation: A Black Working Class* (New York: A. Philip Randolph Institute, 1975).

11. E. Franklin Frazier, *Black Bourgeoisie* (New York: The Free Press, 1957).

12. This assumes, of course, that the distribution of male occupations is an accurate reflection of the class structure in the black community. I have chosen to use the occupation of black males as an indication of the black class structure because it does not compound the problem of male and female from the same household in the labor market. On the other hand, it does not include, of course, the growing numbers of black families headed by females who are also employed. However, when I examined the census data for all employed black workers, the occupational distribution for 1950 changed only slightly (34.2 of black males and females in the working- and middle-class jobs and 65.8 percent in lower-class jobs).

13. In using these figures, I am not implying that intragenerational mobility was widespread, rather these figures most probably reflect intergenerational mobility as more and more new or young workers began having access to an expanding range of jobs.

14. Leonard Broom and Norval D. Glenn, "The Occupations and Incomes of Black Americans," in *Blacks in the United States*, ed. Norval D. Glenn and Charles M. Bonjean (San Francisco: Chandler, 1969), p. 24.

15. U.S. Bureau of the Census, "The Social and Economic Status of the Black Population in the United States, 1974," *Current Population Reports*, Series 23, no. 54 (Washington, D.C.: Government Printing Office, 1975), p. 43. The official low-in-

come, or poverty, threshold for a nonfarm family of four was $2,973 in 1959, $4,540 in 1973, and $5,038 in 1974.

16. Ibid., p. 48.

17. Ibid., p. 11. However, it should be pointed out "that most of the black children not living with both parents were being cared for by at least one parent or by a family member, generally the grandparent" (ibid., p. 4). See also Carol B. Stack, *All Our Kin: Strategies for Survival in a Black Community* (New York: Harper and Row, 1974).

18. For a discussion of this point see Hylan Lewis, "Culture, Class and Family Life among Low Income Urban Negroes," in *Employment, Race, Poverty*, ed. M. Ross and H. Hill (New York: Harcourt, Brace and World, 1967). Also the fact that white women are now entering the labor market in increasing numbers further complicates the job situation for uneducated black males, as they often find themselves competing with better-educated white women for lower-paying but stable employment.

19. Stack, *All Our Kin*, p. 113. Other studies have suggested that rising levels of AFDC payments further increase the rate of female-headed households because the poor are discouraged from entering a marital union if they associate marriage with a drop in real income. See, for example, R. Butler and J. Heckman, "The Impact of the Government on the Labor Market Status of Black Americans: A Critical Review of the Literature and Some New Evidence," manuscript (November 1976).

20. Andrew Brimmer, "Economic Progress of Negroes in the United States: The Deepening Schism" (Paper read at the Founder's Day Convocation, Tuskegee, Alabama, March 22, 1970).

21. Ibid.

22. If we define the black underclass as those below the officially designated low-income level, then 31 percent of the black population (approximately 7.5 million black persons) had this status in 1974, more than triple the comparable percentage for white Americans.

23. John H. Bracey, "Black Nationalism Since Garvey," in *Key Issues in the Afro-American Experience*, p. 267.

24. Peter M. Bergman, *The Chronological History of the Negro in America* (New York: Harper and Row, 1969), p. 509.

25. Martin Kilson, "Black Politicians: A New Power," *Dissent* (August 1971):333–45.

26. See William J. Wilson, *Power, Racism and Privilege: Race Relations in Theoretical and Sociohistorical Perspectives* (New York: The Free Press, 1973); and Castellano B. Turner and William

J. Wilson, "Dimensions of Racial Ideology: A Study of Urban Black Attitudes," *Journal of Social Issues* 32 (Spring 1976):139–52.

27. See, Lewis M. Killian, *White Southerners* (New York: Random House, 1970); and idem, "White Southerners," in *Through Different Eyes: Black and White Perspectives on American Race Relations* ed. Peter I. Rose, Stanley Rothman, and William J. Wilson (New York: Oxford University Press, 1973), pp. 89–113.

28. Wilson, *Power, Racism and Privilege*, chap. 7.

29. Martin Kilson, "Black Politicians: A New Power," *Dissent* (August 1971):333–45.

30. Ibid.

31. "The Social and Economic Status of the Black Population in the United States, 1974," p. 153.

32. See Ira Katznelson, "The Crisis of the Capitalist City: Urban Politics and Social Control," in *Theoretical Perspectives on Urban Politics*, ed. Willis D. Hawley and Michael Lipsky (Englewood Cliffs, N.J.: Prentice-Hall, 1976), pp. 214–29; and John H. Mollenkopf, "The Post-War Politics of Urban Development," *Politics and Society* 5 (1975):247–96.

33. Katznelson, "Crisis of the Capitalist City," p. 219.

34. William C. Baer, "On the Death of Cities," *The Public Interest* 45 (Fall 1976):7–8.

35. Katznelson, "Crisis of the Capitalist City," p. 219.

36. In their analysis of the black middle-income family's opportunity for housing in Chicago, Moore, Livermore, and Galland state: "It can generally buy a house in one of the new developments aimed at blacks. Committees seeking to help black families enter white neighborhoods report more housing opportunities than takers. If a black middle-income family would rather rent, it may be able to do so in a new high-rise development rather than in an old Woodlawn walk up. For the black professional family, to integrate or not to integrate is a live option" (Winston Moore, Charles P. Livermore, and George F. Galland, Jr., "Woodlawn, The Zone of Destruction," *The Public Interest*, 30 [Winter 1973]:41–60). For a discussion of the housing opportunities for blacks and whites in Chicago, see Deborah Haines, "The Black Housing Market in Chicago: A Reassessment of the Filtering Model" (Research and Planning Department, The Urban League of Chicago, March 11, 1977); and Brian J. Berry, "Ghetto Expansion and Housing Prices," Paper prepared for C.U.E. Conference on Economics of the Ghetto, University of Wisconsin, May, 1975.

Chapter Seven

1. The one notable exception is the form of black political subjection imposed by the urban political machines in the earlier twentieth century. However, although the racial developments in the municipal political system had little or no direct or indirect implications for racial interaction in the private industrial sector, some could argue that the systematic exclusion of blacks from meaningful urban participation was a response to the racial antagonisms generated from the social relations of production. Even if one is willing to concede this argument, it could hardly be said that race relations in the urban political system in turn influenced race relations in the private industrial sector.

2. This point is discussed in Chapter 6; see also Richard B. Freeman, *The Over-Educated American* (New York: Academic Press, 1976), chap. 6.

3. U.S. Bureau of the Census, "The Social and Economic Status of the Black Population in the United States, 1974," *Current Population Reports*, Series P–23, no. 54 (Washington, D.C.: Government Printing Office, 1975), p. 42.

BIBLIOGRAPHY

Advisory Commission on Intergovernmental Relations. *Urban America and the Federal System*. Washington, D.C., 1969, M–47.

Averitt, Robert T. *The Dual Economy*. New York: Norton, 1968.

Baer, William C. "On the Death of Cities." *The Public Interest* 45 (Fall 1976):3–19.

Bailey, Harry A., Jr. "Negro Interest Group Strategies." *Urban Affairs Quarterly* 4 (September 1968):27–38.

Baran, Paul A., and Paul M. Sweezy. *Monopoly Capital: An Essay on the American Economic and Social Order*. Harmondsworth, Eng.: Penguin, 1966.

Baron, Harold, and Bennet Hymer. "The Negro in the Chicago Labor Market." In *The Negro and the American Labor Movement*, ed. Julius Jacobsen. New York: Doubleday, Anchor Books, 1968.

Bell, Daniel. *The Coming of Post-Industrial Society: A Venture in Social Forecasting*. New York: Basic Books, 1973.

Bergman, Peter M. *The Chronological History of the Negro in America*. New York: Harper and Row, 1969.

Berlin, Ira. *Slaves without Masters: The Free Negro in the Antebellum South*. New York: Pantheon, 1974.

Berry, Brian J. "Ghetto Expansion and Housing Prices." Paper prepared for C.U.E. Conference on Economics of the Ghetto, University of Wisconsin, May, 1975.

Berwanger, Eugene H. *The Frontier against Slavery: Western Anti-Negro Prejudice and the Slavery Extension Controversy*. Urbana: University of Illinois Press, 1967.

Blassingame, John W. *The Slave Community: Plantation Life in the Ante-Bellum South*. New York: Oxford University Press, 1972.

Bloch, Herman D. *The Circle of Discrimination: An Economic and Social Study of the Black Man in New York*. New York: New York University Press, 1969.

Bluestone, Barry. "Low Wage Industries and the Working Poor." *Poverty and Human Resources Abstracts* 3 (March–April 1968):1–14.

————. "The Tripartite Economy: Labor Markets and the Working Poor." *Poverty and Human Resources* 5 (July–August 1970):15–35.

Blumer, Herbert. "Industrialisation and Race Relations." In *Indus-trialisation and Race Relations: A Symposium*, ed. Guy Hunter. London: Oxford University Press, 1965.

Bonacich, Edna. "Abolition, the Extension of Slavery and the Posi-tion of Free Blacks: A Study of Split Labor Markets in the United States 1830–1863." *American Journal of Sociology* 81 (November 1975):601–28.

————. "Advanced Capitalism and Black-White Relations in the United States: A Split Labor Market Interpretation." *Amer-ican Sociological Review* 41 (February 1976):34–51.

————. "A Theory of Ethnic Antagonism: The Split Labor Mar-ket," *American Sociological Review* 37 (October 1972): 547–59.

Bracey, John H. "Black Nationalism Since Garvey." In *Key Issues in the Afro-American Experience*, ed. Nathan I. Huggins, Martin Kilson, and Daniel M. Fox. New York: Harcourt Brace Jovanovich, 1971.

Brimmer, Andrew, "Economic Progress of Negroes in the United States: The Deepening Schism." Paper read at the Found-er's Day Convocation, Tuskegee, Alabama, March 22, 1970.

————. "Employment and Income in the Black Community: Trends and Outlook." Paper presented under the joint sponsorship of the Committee on Public Lectures, the De-partment of Economics, and the Institute of Government and Public Affairs at the University of California at Los Angeles, California, March 2, 1973.

Brody, David. *Steelworkers in America: The Nonunion Era*. Cam-bridge: Harvard University Press, 1960.

Broom, Leonard, and Norval D. Glenn. "The Occupations and Incomes of Black Americans." In *Blacks in the United States*, ed. Norval D. Glenn and Charles Bonjean. San Francisco: Chandler, 1969.

Bryce-Laporte, Roy Simon. "Slaves as Inmates, Slaves as Men: A Sociological Discussion of Elkins' Thesis." In *The Debate Over Slavery: Stanley Elkins and His Critics*, ed. Ann Lane. Champaign: University of Illinois Press, 1971.

Burawoy, Michael. "Race, Class and Colonialism." *Social and Eco-nomic Studies* 23 (1974):521–50.

Butler, Richard, and James Heckman, *Equal Rights and Industrial Relations*. Madison, Wisconsin: Industrial Relations Re-search Association, 1977.

Chicago Commission on Race Relations. *The Negro in Chicago: A Study of Race Relations and a Race Riot.* Chicago: University of Chicago Press, 1922.

Cloward, Richard A., and Frances Fox Piven. *The Politics of Turmoil: Poverty, Race, and the Urban Crisis.* New York: Vintage Books, 1975.

Congress of the United States. *The Unemployment of Nonwhite Americans; The Effects of Alternative Policies.* Background Paper no. 11. Washington, D.C.: Congressional Budget Office, July 19, 1976.

Conyers, James E., and Walter L. Wallace. *Black Elected Officials: A Study of Black Americans Holding Office.* New York: Russell Sage Foundation, 1976.

Cox, Oliver Cromwell. *Caste, Class and Race: A Study in Social Dynamics.* Garden City, New York: Doubleday, 1948.

Day, Richard H. "Technological Change and the Sharecropper," *American Economic Review* 57 (June 1967):427–49.

Degler, Karl N. "The Irony of American Slavery." In *Perspectives and Irony in American Slavery*, ed. Harry P. Owens. Jackson: University Press of Mississippi, 1976.

Doeringer, Peter B., ed. "Low-Income Labor Markets and Urban Manpower Programs: A Critical Assessment." Report submitted to the Office of Manpower Research. U.S. Department of Labor, January 1969.

————, ed. *Programs to Employ the Disadvantaged.* Englewood Cliffs, N.J.: Prentice-Hall, 1969.

————, and Michael J. Piore. "Equal Employment Opportunity in Boston." *Industrial Relations* 9 (May 1970):324–29.

————. *Internal Labor Markets and Manpower Research.* Report submitted to the Office of Manpower Research, U.S. Department of Labor, 1970.

————, and Michael J. Piore. "Unemployment and the Dual Labor Market." *The Public Interest* 38 (Winter 1975):67–79.

Du Bois, W. E. B. *Black Reconstruction.* New York: Harcourt Brace and Co., 1935.

————. *The Negro Artisan.* Atlanta: Atlanta University Press, 1902.

————. *The Philadelphia Negro: A Social Study.* Political Economy and Public Law Series no. 14. Boston: Ginn, 1899.

Elkins, Stanley M. "On Slavery and Ideology." In *The Debate Over Slavery: Stanley Elkins and His Critics*, ed. by Ann Lane. Champaign: University of Illinois Press, 1971.

————. *Slavery: A Problem in American Institutional and Intellectual Life.* Chicago: University of Chicago Press, 1959.

————. "The Social Consequences of Slavery." In *Key Issues in the Afro-American Experience,* ed. Nathan I. Huggins, Martin Kilson, and Daniel M. Fox. New York: Harcourt Brace Jovanovich, 1971.

Farley, Reynolds. *Growth of the Black Population: A Study of Demographic Trends.* Chicago: Markham Publishing Co., 1970.

Ferman, Louis A. "The Irregular Economy: Informal Work Patterns in the Ghetto." Mimeographed. University of Michigan, 1967.

Fishel, Leslie H., Jr., and Benjamin Quarles. *The Negro American: A Documentary History.* Glenview, Ill.: Scott, Foresman, 1967.

Fogel, Robert William, and Stanley L. Engerman. *Time on the Cross: The Economics of American Negro Slavery.* Boston: Little, Brown, 1974.

Fogel, Walter A. *The Negro in the Meat-Packing Industry.* Philadelphia: University of Pennsylvania Press, 1970.

Foner, Eric. *Free Soil, Free Labor, Free Men: The Ideology of the Republican Party before the Civil War.* New York: Oxford University Press, 1970.

Foner, Philip S. *History of the Labor Movement in the United States,* vol. 1. New York: International Publishers, 1947.

Foster, William Z. *The Great Steel Strike and Its Lessons.* New York: Da Capo Press, 1971.

Franklin, John Hope. *From Slavery to Freedom.* 3d ed. New York: Alfred A. Knopf, 1967.

Frazier, E. Franklin. *Black Bourgeoisie.* New York: The Free Press, 1957.

————. *The Negro in the United States.* New York: Macmillan, 1957.

Frederickson, George M. "The Gutman Report." *New York Review of Books* 23, no. 15 (September 3, 1976):18–22, 27.

————. "Toward a Social Interpretation of the Development of American Racism." In *Key Issues in the Afro-American Experience,* ed. Nathan I. Huggins, Martin Kilson, and Daniel Fox. New York: Harcourt Brace Jovanovich, 1971.

Freeman, Richard B. "Changes in the Labor Market for Black Americans, 1948–72." In *Brookings Papers on Economic Activity* 1 (1973):67–120.

————. "The Implications of the Changing Labor Market for Members of Minority Groups." In *Higher Education and* the *Labor Market*, ed. Margaret G. Gordon. New York: McGraw-Hill, 1973.

———. *The Over-Educated American.* New York: Academic Press, 1976.

Friedlander, Stanley L. *Unemployment in the Urban Core.* New York: Praeger, 1972.

Friedman, Murray. "The Jews." In *Through Different Eyes: Black and White Perspectives on American Race Relations,* ed. Peter I. Rose, Stanley Rothman, and William J. Wilson. New York: Oxford University Press, 1973.

Fusfeld, Daniel R. *The Basic Economics of the Urban Racial Crisis.* New York: Holt, Rinehart and Winston, 1973.

Gans, Herbert J. "The Ghetto Rebellions and Urban Class Conflict." In *Urban Riots,* ed. Robert Connery. New York: Proceedings of the Academy of Political Science, 1969.

Genovese, Eugene D. *In Red and Black: Marxian Explorations in Southern and Afro-American History.* New York: Vintage Press, 1971.

———. *The Political Economy of Slavery: Studies in the Economy and Society of the Slave South.* New York: Pantheon, 1966.

———. *Roll, Jordan, Roll: The World the Slaves Made.* New York: Pantheon, 1974.

———. *The World the Slaveholders Made: Two Essays in Interpretation.* New York: Pantheon, 1969.

Glazer, Nathan. "Blacks and Ethnic Groups: The Difference, and the Political Difference It Makes." In *Key Issues in the Afro-American Experience,* ed. Nathan I. Huggins, Martin Kilson, and Daniel M. Fox. New York: Harcourt Brace Jovanovich, 1971.

Gordon, David M. "Income and Welfare in New York City." *The Public Interest,* no. 16 (Summer 1969):64–101.

———. *Theories of Poverty and Underemployment.* Lexington, Mass.: D. C. Heath, 1972.

Gordon, Milton M. *Assimilation in American Life.* New York: Oxford University Press, 1964.

Gosnell, Harold F. *Machine Politics: Chicago Model.* 2d ed. Chicago: University of Chicago Press, 1968.

Gutman, Herbert G. *The Black Family in Slavery and Freedom, 1750–1925.* New York: Pantheon, 1976.

Haines, Deborah. "The Black Housing Market in Chicago: A Reassessment of the Filtering Model." Research and Planning Department, The Urban League of Chicago, March 11, 1977.

Hamilton, C. Horace. "The Negro Leaves the South," *Demography*, no. 1 (1964):273–95.

Hare, Nathan. *Black Anglo-Saxons*. New York: Collier, 1965.

Harris, Marvin. *Patterns of Race in the Americas*. New York: Walker, 1964.

Hashimoto, Masanore, and Jacob Mincer. "Employment and Unemployment Effects of Minimum Wages." In *The NBER Report on Research in Labor Markets for USLD*. National Bureau of Economic Research, 1972.

Herbst, Alma. "The Negro in the Slaughtering and Meat Packing Industry in Chicago." Ph.D. dissertation. University of Chicago, 1930.

Hummel, Raymond C., and John M. Nagel. *Urban Education in America: Problems and Prospects*. New York: Oxford University Press, 1973.

Janowitz, Morris. "Patterns of Collective Racial Violence." In *Violence in America: Historical and Comparative Perspectives*, ed. Hugh Davis Graham and Ted Robert Gurr. New York: Bantam Books, 1969.

————. *Social Control of the Welfare State*. New York: Elsevier, 1976.

Kahn, Tom. "Problems of the Negro Movement." *Dissent* (Winter 1964):108–38.

Kain, John F. "The Distribution and Movement of Jobs and Industry." In *The Metropolitan Enigma: Inquiries into the Nature and Dimension of America's "Urban Crisis,"* ed. James Q. Wilson. Cambridge: Harvard University Press, 1968.

Katznelson, Ira. *Black Men, White Cities: Race Politics and Migration in the United States, 1900–30, and Britain, 1948–68*. London: Oxford University Press, 1973.

————. "The Crisis of the Capitalist City: Urban Politics and Social Control." In *Theoretical Perspectives on Urban Politics*, ed. Willis D. Hawley and Michael Lipsky. Englewood Cliffs, N.J.: Prentice-Hall, 1976.

————. "Introduction." *Race: A Journal of Race and Group Relations* 14 (April 1973):v–vi.

Key, V. O. Jr. *Southern Politics in State and Nation*. New York: Alfred A. Knopf, 1949.

Kidder, Alice Handsaker. "Racial Difference in Job Search and Wages." *Monthly Labor Review* 91 (July 1968):24–26.

Killian, Lewis, M. *White Southerners*. New York: Random House, 1970.

————. "White Southerners." In *Through Different Eyes: Black and White Perspectives on American Race Relations*, ed. Peter I. Rose, Stanley Rothman, and William J. Wilson. New York: Oxford University Press, 1973.

Killingsworth, Charles C., Jr. "The Continuing Labor Market Twist." *Monthly Labor Review* 91 (September 1968):12–17.

————. *Jobs and Income for Negroes*. Ann Arbor: University of Michigan Press, 1968.

Kilson, Martin. "Black Politicians: A New Power." *Dissent* (August 1971):333–45.

————. "Political Change in the Negro Ghetto, 1900–1940." In *Key Issues in the Afro-American Experience*, ed. Nathan I. Huggins, Martin Kilson, and Daniel M. Fox. New York: Harcourt Brace Jovanovich, 1971.

Kosters, Marvin and Finis Welch, "The Effects of Minimum Wages by Race, Sex and Age." In *Racial Discrimination in Economic Life*, ed. Anthony Pascal. Lexington, Mass.: Lexington Books, 1972.

Lane, Ann, ed. *The Debate Over Slavery: Stanley Elkins and His Critics*. Champaign: University of Illinois Press, 1971.

Lewis, Hylan. "Culture, Class and Family Life Among Low Income Urban Negroes." In *Employment, Race, Poverty*, ed. M. Ross and H. Hill. New York: Harcourt, Brace and World, 1967.

Liebow, Elliot. *Tally's Corner: A Study of Negro Streetcorner Men*. Boston: Little, Brown, 1967.

Litwack, Leon F. *North of Slavery: The Negro in the Free States, 1790–1860*. Chicago: University of Chicago Press, 1961.

Lofton, Williston. "Abolition and Labor." *The Journal of Negro History* 33 (July 1948):249–93.

————. "Northern Labor and the Negro during the Civil War." *The Journal of Negro History* 34 (July 1949):251–73.

Lynch, Hollis R. *The Black Urban Condition: A Documentary History, 1866–1971*. New York: Thomas Y. Crowell, 1973.

Man, Albon P., Jr. "Labor Competition and the New York Draft Riots of 1863." *The Journal of Negro History* 36 (October 1951):375–405.

Mandel, Bernard. *Labor: Free and Slave; Workingmen and the Anti-Slavery Movement in the United States*. New York: Associated Authors, 1955.

Marshall, Ray. "Industrialisation and Race Relations in the Southern United States." In *Industrialisation and Race Relations*, ed. Guy Hunter. London: Oxford University Press, 1961.

————. *The Negro and Organized Labor.* New York: John Wiley and Sons, 1965.

————. *The Negro Worker.* New York: Random House, 1967.

Meier, August, and Elliott Rudwick. *From Plantation to Ghetto: An Interpretive History of the American Negro.* Rev. ed. New York: Hill and Wang, 1970.

Mollenkopf, John H. "The Post-War Politics of Urban Development." *Politics and Society* 5 (1975):247–96.

Moon, Henry L. *Balance of Power: The Negro Vote.* Garden City, New York: Doubleday, 1948.

Moore, Thomas Gale. "The Effects of Minimum Wages on Teenage Unemployment Rates." *Journal of Political Economy* 79 (July–August 1971):897–902.

Moore, Winston, Charles P. Livermore, and George F. Galland, Jr. "Woodlawn: The Zone of Destruction." *The Public Interest* 30 (Winter 1973):41–60.

Morgan, Edmund S. *American Slavery, American Freedom: The Ordeal of Colonial Virginia.* New York: W. W. Norton, 1975.

Morris, Richard B. *Government and Labor in Early America.* New York: Octagon, 1965.

Myrdal, Gunnar. *An American Dilemma: The Negro Problem and Modern Democracy.* New York: Harper and Row, 1944.

National Advisory Commission on Civil Disorders. *Report of the National Advisory Commission on Civil Disorders.* New York: Bantam Books, 1968.

Nikolinakos, M. "Notes on an Economic Theory of Racism." *Race: A Journal of Race and Group Relations* 14 (April 1973): 365–81.

O'Connor, James. *The Fiscal Crisis of the State.* New York: St. Martin's Press, 1973.

Osofsky, Gilbert. *Harlem: The Making of a Ghetto, 1830–1930.* New York: Harper, 1966.

Owens, Carmen J. "Power, Racism and Coalition Politics: A Reexamination of the Populist Movement in Georgia." Master's thesis, University of Chicago, 1973.

Piore, Michael J. "On the Job Training and the Dual Labor Market." In *Public-Private Manpower Policies,* ed. Arnold Weber et al. Madison, Wisconsin: Industrial Relations Research Association, 1969.

————. "Negro Workers in the Mississippi Delta: Problems of Displacement and Adjustment." *Proceedings of the Industrial Research Association* (Winter 1967):366–74.

———. "The Dual Labor Market: Theory and Implications." *Problems in Political Economy: An Urban Perspective*, ed. David M. Gordon. Lexington, Mass.: D. C. Heath, 1971.

Quarles, Benjamin. *The Negro in the Making of America*. New York: Collier Books, 1964.

Reich, Michael. "The Economics of Racism." *Problems of Political Economy*, ed. David M. Gordon. Lexington, Mass.: D. C. Heath, 1971.

Reid, Ira De A. *Negro Membership in American Labor Unions*. New York: Negro Universities Press, 1969.

Reissman, Leonard. "Readiness to Succeed: Mobility Aspirations and Modernism Among the Poor." *Urban Affairs Quarterly* 4 (March 1969):387–95.

Rex, John. "The Concept of Race in Sociological Theory." In *Race and Racialism*, ed. Sami Zubaida. London: Tavistock Publications, 1970.

Rudwick, Elliott M. *Race Riot at East St. Louis*. Carbondale: Southern Illinois University Press, 1964.

Russell, Robert R. *Economic Aspects of Southern Sectionalism*. Urbana: University of Illinois Press, 1923.

Rustin, Bayard. *The Foundation: A Black Working Class*. New York: A. Philip Randolph Institute, 1975.

Schluter, Herman. *Labor and Slavery: A Chapter from the Social History of America*. New York: Socialist Literature Company, 1913.

Scruggs, Otis M. "The Economic and Racial Components of Jim Crow." In *Key Issues in the Afro-American Experience*, ed. Nathan I. Huggins, Martin Kilson, and Daniel M. Fox. New York: Harcourt Brace Jovanovich, 1971.

Shugg, Roger W. *Origins of Class Struggle in Louisiana*. Baton Rouge: Louisiana State University Press, 1939.

Smelser, Neil J. *Karl Marx on Society and Social Change*. Chicago: University of Chicago Press, 1974.

Spear, Allen. "The Origins of the Urban Ghetto, 1870–1915." In *Key Issues in the Afro-American Experience*, ed. Nathan I. Huggins, Martin Kilson, and Daniel M. Fox. New York: Harcourt Brace Jovanovich, 1971.

Spero, Sterling D., and Abram L. Harris. *The Black Worker*. New York: Columbia University Press, 1931.

Stack, Carol B. *All Our Kin: Strategies for Survival in a Black Community*. New York: Harper and Row, 1974.

Stampp, Kenneth M. *The Peculiar Institution: Slavery in the Ante-Bellum South*. New York: Alfred A. Knopf, 1956.

Starobin, Robert S. *Industrial Slavery in the Old South*. New York: Oxford University Press, 1970.

Thornbrough, Emma Lou. *The Negro in Indiana in 1900: A Study of a Minority*. Indiana Historical Collections, vol. 37. Indianapolis: Indiana Historical Bureau, 1957.

Tocqueville, Alexis de. *Democracy in America*, ed. J. P. Mayer. New York: Doubleday, 1969.

Turner, Castellano B., and William J. Wilson. "Dimensions of Racial Ideology: A Study of Urban Black Attitudes." *Journal of Social Issues* 32 (Spring 1976):139–52.

Turner, Louis. *Multinational Corporations and the Third World*. New York: Hill and Wang, 1973.

Tuttle, William M., Jr. "Labor Conflict and Racial Violence: The Black Worker in Chicago, 1849–1919." *Labor History* 10 (Summer 1969):408–32.

U.S. Bureau of Labor Statistics. "Youth Unemployment and Minimum Wages," Bulletin 1657. Washington, D.C.: Government Printing Office, 1970.

U.S. Bureau of the Census. *Census of the Population*. Washington, D.C.: Government Printing Office, 1940, 1950, 1960, 1970.

————. "The Social and Economic Status of the Black Population in the United States, 1973." In *Current Population Reports*. Series P–23, no. 48. Washington, D.C.: Government Printing Office, July 1974.

————. "The Social and Economic Status of the Black Population in the United States, 1974. In *Current Population Reports*. Series P–23, no. 54. Washington, D.C.: Government Printing Office, July 1975.

U.S. Department of Labor. *Handbook of Labor Statistics*. Washington, D.C.: Government Printing Office, 1975.

————. *Manpower Report of the President*. Washington, D.C.: Government Printing Office, annual reports for 1972, 1973, 1975.

U.S. Government. *Economic Report of the President*. Washington, D.C.: Government Printing Office, 1975.

van den Berghe, Pierre. *Race and Racism: A Comparative Perspective*. New York: John Wiley and Sons, 1967.

Vander Horst, Sheila T. "The Effects of Industrialisation on Race Relations in South Africa." In *Industrialisation and Race Relations: A Symposium*, ed. Guy Hunter. London: Oxford University Press, 1965.

Vietorisz, Thomas, and Bennet Harrison. *The Economic Development of Harlem.* New York: Praeger, 1970.

Voegeli, V. Jacque. *Free but Not Equal: The Midwest and the Negro during the Civil War.* Chicago: University of Chicago Press, 1967.

Wachtel, Howard M. "The Impact of Labor Market Conditions on Hard-Core Unemployment: A Case Study of Detroit." *Poverty and Human Resources* 5 (July–August 1968):5–13.

Wachter, Michael L. "Primary and Secondary Labor Markets: A Critique of the Dual Approach." *Brookings Papers on Economic Activity* 4 (1974):637–81.

Wade, Richard C. *Slavery in the Cities: The South 1820–1860.* New York: Oxford University Press, 1964.

Welks, Paul, "The White Ethnics." In *Through Different Eyes: Black and White Perspectives on American Race Relations,* ed. Peter I. Rose, Stanley Rothman, and William J. Wilson. New York: Oxford University Press, 1973.

Whitfield, T. M. *Slavery Agitation in Virginia, 1792–1832.* Baltimore: Johns Hopkins University Press, 1930.

Wilhelm, Sidney M. *Who Needs the Negro?* Cambridge, Mass.: Schenkman Publishing Co., 1970.

Wilkinson, Doris, and Ronald L. Taylor, eds. *The Black Male in America: Perspectives on His Status in Contemporary Society.* Chicago: Nelson-Hall, 1977.

Wilson, William J. *Power, Racism and Privilege: Race Relations in Theoretical and Sociohistorical Perspectives.* New York: The Free Press, 1973..

——. "Race Relations Models and Ghetto Behavior." In *Nation of Nations: The Ethnic Experience and the Racial Crisis,* ed. Peter I. Rose. New York: Random House, 1972.

——. "The Significance of Social and Racial Prisms." In *Through Different Eyes: Black and White Perspectives on American Race Relations,* ed. Peter I. Rose, Stanley Rothman, and William J. Wilson. New York: Oxford University Press, 1973.

——, and Vernon Gray. "The Application of the Colonial Model to the Black Community." Paper presented at the annual meeting of the American Sociological Association, Denver, Colorado, August 1971.

——, and Katherine O'Sullivan See. "School Desegregation and Structural Changes in the Economy." Paper presented at the annual meeting of the American Sociological Association, New York City, August 1976.

Woodward, C. Vann. *American Counterpoint: Slavery and Racism in the North-South Dialogue*. Boston: Little, Brown, 1971.

————. *Origins of the New South, 1877–1913*. Baton Rouge: Louisiana State University Press, 1951.

————. *Tom Watson: An Agrarian Rebel:* New York: Oxford University Press, 1938.

Young, Donald. *American Minority Peoples: A Study in Racial and Cultural Conflicts in the United States*. New York: Harper, 1932.

Zilversmit, Arthur. *The First Emancipation: The Abolition of Slavery in the North*. Chicago: University of Chicago Press, 1967.

INDEX